UNCOMMON MEDITATIONS

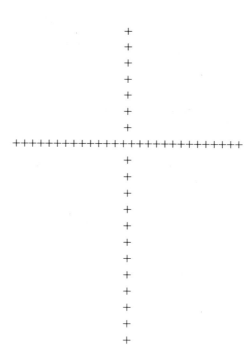

THE CROSS AND PARADISE ON EARTH

JAMES F. LA CROCE

Also by the Author

ESCAPE FROM HELL AND THE ALMIGHTY WHITE GUY WITH A BEARD

JESUS, MAN ON A MISSION

Bible quotes are not cited as proofs
but as passages which have graced my life in Jesus.

Other quotes are often cited
to make my point, not the author's.

1621416666
ISBN

AUTHOR'S GRATITUDE

My thanks to the Glen Rock, NJ
Writers' Group for their helpful
observations and encouraging comments.

TO JESUS OF GALILEE

One of the thousands of Jews crucified by Rome

If no angels were cast into hell
(presuming no one can sin in heaven)

If no one named Adam and Eve disobeyed God
(presuming we are not born as sinners)

If the evil we do trespasses one another not God
(as you presumed when you taught us to pray)

If there is no wrath of God, no hell
(as presumed by many today)

Why were you crucified?
Who benefited from your death?

Cui Bono?

Meditation Prompt

"It is the best possible time to be alive,
when almost everything you know
is wrong."

Tom Stoppard

Author's Presumptions

The Bible and Christianity

The bible is a book of sacred and inspiring stories
of the religious experiences of two faith communities
told in primitive and patriarchal times.
In those days it was believed God "spoke" only to men.
(That in itself should tell you something.)

The Christian Church is a house-divided
and as such cannot stand.
It has dared to proclaim God rejected the Jews
while assuming his son will not reject the Christians.

Meditating with these presumptions in mind
may not lead you to where I am in my faith
but they may help you reflect on where you are,
and that would be a grace beyond measure.

For Jim Coriden and Charlie Curran:
uncommon theologians,
faithful servants,
prolific scholars.

For married priests and nuns:
ministers without portfolio,
and the laity they serve,
dispersed but not dismayed.

For my nephew, Jim, and his partner Matthew:
may the grace of God
continue to prevail
in their relational orientation.

For myself:
too soon old, too late smart,
far too long a pale rider
riding the pale horse of personal salvation.

TABLE OF CONTENTS

PREQUEL xi

PREFACE..xiii

PROLOGUE.. xv

PERSONAL TESTIMONY...xvii

BOOK ONE - THE CROSS: GALILEE TO CHRISTIANITY.......... 1

    Chapter One - Jesus in Galilee: No Ordinary Time 5

    Chapter Two - Jesus on the cross: His very last words? 18

    Chapter Three - Looking at the Cross, what do I see? 34

    Chapter Four - A Cross Examination...77

    Chapter Five - Christianity: Back to Ordinary Time...................88

BOOK TWO - PARADISE: OUR FATHER'S KINGDOM ON

    EARTH 99

    Chapter Six - Jesus in his Public Square..................................102

    Chapter Seven - Jesus in our Public Square.............................121

    Chapter Eight - Christianity in our Public Square....................131

    Chapter Nine - Jesus' Public Square Parables 165

EPILOGUE - NATHAN AND PAUL 200

APPENDIX 205

PREQUEL

In our creeds and doctrines we gave Jesus a job
only he could do – save us from the legendary wrath of God.

In his ministry and his parables Jesus gave us a job
only we could do – usher in the legendary kingdom of God on earth.

In our Christian faith down through the ages
the job Jesus gave us counted for little.

His "kingdom come" prayer to Our Father
is but a piety that never made it into our creeds.

Who can blame us? The kingdom on earth will not come
unless we treat the least as if they were Jesus.

Saving our souls is no walk in the park.
But it is nothing compared to saving our world.

Accepting the kingdom on earth job may do little to change the world,
but it will do a world of good for our spirituality.

Meditation Prompt

I do not count my mother's life of faith and my upbringing in traditional Roman Catholicism as flapping about in spiritual garbage. I count as a blessing the faith that brought my mother through hard times and led me to where I am today.

But in the twilight of my life, in my eighty-third year, I must agree with C.S. Lewis:

"For I cannot help thinking that any religion which begins with a thirst for immortality is damned as a religion, from the outset. Until a certain spiritual level has been reached, the promise of Immortality will always operate as a bribe which vitiates the whole religion, infinitely inflames those very self-regards which religion must cut down and uproot...."

PREFACE

In 1941 a German New Testament professor published a book entitled: "Jesus kein Jude war." ("Jesus was not a Jew.") The man on the cross, he claimed, was more Greek than Jewish. It could not be otherwise. Greek culture was enlightened, while the Semitic culture was backward.

This book was more propaganda than scholarship.

In 1991, a professor at Catholic University of America in Washington published a book entitled "A Marginal Jew." He introduced his work by imagining a Catholic, a Protestant, a Jewish and an Agnostic Scholar were locked in the Harvard library. They were not allowed to emerge until they reached a consensus on Jesus. His book suggested they might very well agree that Jesus was a marginal Jew.

This book was more scholarship than the laity could handle.

In the decades between the German and American publications a Dutchman and two Germans, three reputable theologians, posed the crucial question about Jesus: WHY was he a CRUCIFIED Jew? They proposed that he was crucified because of his freely chosen ministry in Galilee.

This response promised bright beginnings.

In their brave new Christian theology we would no longer revere the crucified Jesus as a victim of divine wrath. Nor would we live as if his few years of lifting up the lowly and putting down the mighty counted for little, almost nothing, compared to his few hours on the cross. Jesus was not born to be crucified but to be a prophet for a kingdom on earth. He risked everything for a dream that Christianity has yet to dream.

This brave new theology is still a mustard seed.

This one big step in theology could have been one great leap for Christianity, each Parish committed to ushering in the kingdom on earth.

But Rome was not pleased with this disregard for heaven and hell. Nor would most of the laity have been edified if these publications had ever reached the pulpits. But to give Rome and the laity their due, this bright beginning cast a shadow over Christianity's most cherished tradition: if the crucifixion did not save Christians from hell and Satan, how then is Jesus our Savior; from what have we been saved?

But in light of the diminishing role of hell in sermons and theological discourse a Christian can rightly ask: was Jesus crucified because of his mission? Did he die to satisfy the wrath of Pilate, not the wrath of God? Was it his mission of ushering in the kingdom on earth and not Adam's sin in the garden of paradise that nailed him to the cross?

What cross does Jesus expect us to carry? Is it the cross he carried, the cross of service to the least? If so, it is no wonder that Christianity is a house divided and the world is in such a mess.

PROLOGUE

In 1929 I was baptized in the Roman Catholic Church.
I was taught to begin and end every prayer with the sign of the cross.
I believed the cross was all about God's love for Catholics.

My last name, La Croce, means "the cross".
It was great to be a Roman Catholic named La Croce.
"La Croce" saved me from the holy wrath of God, the unholy power of Satan.
In my childish imagination a cross was planted at the gates of heaven and hell.
On both crosses was nailed this terrorist threat:
Abandon all hope ye who are not Catholics

That this cross sent most of humanity to hell mattered little to me.
Even if it did, what could I do?
Jesus gave the keys of the kingdom of heaven to Peter.

At worship our mass re-enacted the crucifixion.
At worship the Protestants only "remembered" the crucifixion.
They believed that the Friday crucifixion needed no ritual repeats.
The blood shed that day saved true blue Protestants from hell.
Who they may be is being debated even as I write.

In their childish imagination a cross was planted at the gates of heaven and hell.
On each cross was nailed this terrorist threat:
Abandon all hope ye who are not Protestants

Still, Catholics were as bad off as the Protestants and the rest of humanity.
Any un-confessed mortal sin sent us straight to hell.

Our mortal sin list went on and on. It included birth control and eating meat on Friday. All this sounds sinister I know. But they say it really is so.

I do not count my upbringing as garbage time but as a time of grace. But my faith would have been better served by a church calling me to take up the cross of Jesus' ministry to the wretched, to revere Jesus as a son sent on a mission not as a son born to be crucified.

I no longer believe all I was taught as a child.
I am not an ex-catholic or anti-catholic.
I am a retired catholic, living on my uncommon meditations.
There was only one passion that urged me on:

"I wanted to see what was there for me once, what is there for me now."

Lillian Hellman

PERSONAL TESTIMONY

Surprised by grace

Since retiring from teaching I had been pondering the dark side of Christianity. Then one Sunday morning I experienced the glory of our faith.

While visiting some Presbyterian friends I attended Sunday worship with them. I was deeply moved by the fervor of the Congregation's full throated and emotionally charged singing of the hymn "In Christ's Love My Hope Is Found."

The Congregation was brimming with great expectations as it sang: "This wrong, this worry, I put in your hands."

I was caught up in the awesome and overwhelming power of our faith. Not one by one, but as one body, we sang our burdens into Christ's hands. To sing your prayer is to pray twice, said Augustine. Singing as a Congregation is the fullness of grace.

There is nothing dark and sinister about this tradition.
The Jews embrace it on Saturdays and the Muslims on Fridays.
Their "Christs" or "anointed ones" are Moses and Mohammed.
They, too, go to God brimming with great expectations.

That's what makes religion so popular – and prosperous.

But then I was surprised by grace. I heard Jesus singing to me the very same hymn I was singing to him.

On his back was a sick, naked, hungry, thirsty, outlaw black woman.
His eyes were flooded with tears as he sang:
"This wrong, this worry, this burden, this hope, I put in your hands.
I have been carrying her for 2,000 years. I need your help!"

xvii

Jesus, Mary and holy St. Joseph, have pity on me, I prayed.
Neither Creed nor Country taught me to put this woman on my back.
I never did that. I cannot do it now. I am eighty years old for god's
sake.

Not to worry said Jesus. My surprise visit is not about guilt.
Guilt is a sinister emotion posing as a virtue. It has none of the grace
of grief and regret for harm done to self or others.
Do what you can. Do more than you are doing now.
But at least stir up a little anger about what was given to you.

This book of uncommon meditations is the best I can do for the sick,
naked, hungry, outlaw, black woman on the back of Jesus.

There is in these meditations an undercurrent of anger.

Practicing Meditation

In relating to God
listening is always
more graceful
than talking.

Let us not belittle
the power of the listening
that helps us see why
we do not live more wisely.

In reading about God
reading with an open mind
is always more graceful
than reading defensively.

I know this
from personal experience,
and most likely,
you do, too.

"It is only in and through people,
inwardly developed men and women,
that God can exist and act
in the world of man on earth."

Jacob Needleman

James F. La Croce

"If Christianity is dying
could it not be
to bring forth a new humanity
which will need us as midwives?"

John Kaiser

BOOK ONE
THE CROSS:
GALILEE TO CHRISTIANITY

"Jesus promised us the kingdom on earth
and all we got was the church."

Loisy

Author's Alert

Jesus was super "natural".

He came into this world
in the most natural way,
no nurses and doctors attending.

He went about his business
not by trains, planes or automobiles,
but by using the feet God gave him.

He ate and drank as we do
but voided both without the luxury
of our bathroom facilities.

He lived most of his life
as an anonymous Jew,
making no impression on anyone.

He believed it to be a wise decision
to live on earth as a human person
and so teach us the path to paradise on earth.

He may or may not have walked on water
but it was by walking the roads of Galilee
that he preached the kingdom on earth.

What could be more natural
than walking, arguing, winning, and losing,
trying to make planet earth a better world?

Book One: The Cross: Galilee to Christianity

Chapter 1. Jesus in Galilee: No Ordinary Time

Chapter 2. Jesus on the Cross: His Very Last Words

Chapter 3. Looking at the Cross: What Do I See?

Chapter 4. A Cross Examination: Shades of Grey

Chapter 5. Christianity: Back to Ordinary Time

"Biblically speaking it is more accurate to say
Jesus is the revelation of God rather than Jesus is God."

Ray Brown

"As long as we perform our works
in order to go to heaven,
we are simply on the wrong track."

Eckhart

Chapter One
Jesus in Galilee: No Ordinary Time

What Winston Churchill said
about the time the Allies invaded North Africa
can rightly be said about the time Jesus invaded Northern Palestine.

"Now this is not the end...
It is not even the beginning of the end.
But it is the end of the beginning."

Meditations: Jesus in Galilee: No Ordinary Time

1. No Ordinary Man

2. No Ordinary Baptism

3. No Ordinary Creed

4. No Ordinary Mission

5. No Ordinary Community

"The true mystery of the world
is the visible not the invisible."

Oscar Wilde

1. MEDITATION

No Ordinary Man

He was a unique incarnation of God.
But he lived thirty years as an anonymous Jew.

He was a teacher and a prophet.
But he put nothing in writing, not even a word.

He is one of the most revered men in history.
But the facts about him would not fill a page.

His good news has spread throughout the world.
But he preached it only within thirty miles of his home town.

He is revered as a Lord.
But he lived more as a servant.

He went about as a man with authority.
But he did not believe in "lording."

He had no problem with insubordination.
There were no subordinates.

He went out to the wretched.
For him, they were the Temple of the Holy Spirit.

His faith and piety was unlike that of his followers today.
He favored deeds over creeds, justice over rituals, empathy over efficiency.

He accepted a mission that was risky business.
Some would call it Mission Impossible.

But he planted his feet wide and stood tall.
He walked the line.

Meditation Prompt

"I believe in jesus christ...
who couldn't beat City Hall,
worked to change the status quo
and was destroyed.

Looking at him I see how
our intelligence is crippled,
our imagination stifled,
our efforts wasted
because we did not live as he did."

Dorothy Soelle

2. MEDITATION

No Ordinary Baptism

Jesus was baptized in a congregation of Jews,
in preparation for the coming kingdom of God.

His baptism was one of repentance for personal sins,
and for this his Father was well pleased.

Jesus was all fired up as he began his ministry,
and he baptized with fire and spirit, not with water:

"The Spirit has sent me
to bring glad tidings to the poor..."
(Luke 4: 18)

His fellow Nazarenes were not pleased.
They had heard this sermon before from other prophets.

Being baptized into serving the poor
is not for the faint-hearted.

Lifting up the lowly as did Jesus,
often meant putting down the mighty.

Jesus' eyes were on the kingdom of heaven on earth as the prize.
Our eyes are on the kingdom of heaven in heaven as the prize.

Meditation Prompt

"As you go, proclaim the good news,
'The kingdom of heaven has come near…
You received without payment…
give without payment.'"

Matthew 10:7-8

3. MEDITATION

No Ordinary Creed

The Lord's Creed:

I believe in relating to God as Our Father, not as My Father.
"Almighty" means nothing to me. I take no note of it.

I believe the kingdom on earth will hallow my Father's name.
Heaven means nothing to my mission. I take no note of it.

I believe the kingdom will come when bread is on every table.
I take no note of bread that is not worthy of the Father's table.

I believe Our Father's name is blasphemed when he is feared.
I take no note of hell or wrath in my creed.

I believe nothing we can do offends our Father.
I take no note of sin in my creed.

I believe that the evil we do offends others.
I take note that we are forgiven only as we forgive.

I believe in God as described in the parable of the Prodigal Son.
I take no note of a Judge who goes by the book.

I believe in the Parable of the Judgment of the Nations.
I take no note of Christianity's go-to-hell sin lists.

Meditation Prompt

Seamus and Herman,
lend me your words in trying to do justice
to the Lord's Creed:

"And now this is an inheritance –
upright, rudimentary, unshiftably planked
in the long ago, yet willable forward
again and again and again."

Seamus Heaney

"Give me a condor's quill!
Give me Vesuvius' crater for an ink stand/'"

Herman Melville

4. MEDITATION

No Ordinary Mission

Jesus went through Galilee
like a needle pulling thread,
weaving the wretched and poor
into a seamless garment.

The thread was his mighty works;
nothing pleased the wretched more:
keep it coming they chanted,
much to the dismay of Jesus.

The needle was his parables;
nothing annoyed them more
than getting the needle,
much to the dismay of Jesus.

Jesus in the kingdom of Caesar
was a thorn in Pilate's side,
a Galilee without the wretched
is an economy without cheap labor.

Mind your own business, Pilate warned.
Taking care of the poor is my business.
Not if I have anything to say about it, said Jesus.
Not on my watch.

You ask too much of us, Christians lament.
Taking care of the poor is a piety not a creed.
We can do little more for the poor
than do other social organizations.

I'm looking at you,
yes, you, said Jesus;
don't you dare look away,
don't you dare.

Meditation Prompt

"I'm always a little surprised
to find my eyebrows unsinged
after I've suffered one of those looks."

Marilynne Robinson

5. MEDITATION

No Ordinary Community

Q. What were the followers of Jesus first called?

A. They were first called *The People of the Way.*
In Acts 9:2, Paul was sent to arrest any who belonged to *The Way.*
In Acts 19:23, the riot in Ephesus was about *The Way.*

Q. What was meant by *The* Way?

A. No one really knows but it very likely was the way the Jerusalem Community held everything in common and gave highest community priority to providing for the poor. (Acts 4:32-37)
The story is told of two members of the community struck dead by God because they held back some of the money to be given to the poor. (Acts 5: 1-11)

This incredible story, not to be taken literally, suggests that there was a Jerusalem Community whose rock of faith was the Community's commitment to the poor. These followers of Jesus were not yet known as Christians.

Q When did the *People of The Way* become known as *Christians?*

A. When Jesus' last parable was no longer the rock on which each community was founded, when Paul preached Jesus Christ crucified as the power and wisdom of God, when the Jesus movement shifted from East to West and from Jews to Gentiles.
Q. What became of *The People of the Way?*
A. There is no record of their story. History never favors the losers.
The story of those to whom Jesus ministered in Galilee has never been told.

15

The Galileans to whom Jesus preached gave way to the Gentiles to whom Paul preached.
The kingdom on earth mission gave way to the kingdom of heaven mission.
What Jesus can do for his followers won out over what they could do for Jesus.

Whether Christianity did right by Paul is another question.
Without him who knows what would have happened to the Jesus movement?
The mission of Jesus in Galilee and Judea died not long after he died.
What would Jesus say, what were his expectations?

Meditation Prompt

Jesus: Great Expectations

"Where Jesus lives, the great-hearted gather.
We are a door that's never locked.
If you are suffering any kind of pain,
stand near this door. Open it."

Rumi

Meditation Prompt for chapter one

Jesus in Galilee: No Ordinary Time

"Of this treachery who could be the author?"

Mozart
"La Clemenza di Tito"

Chapter Two
Jesus on the cross: His very last words?

"My God, my God, why have you forsaken me?
(Mark 15:34 and Matthew 27:46)

OR

"Father, into thy hands I commend my spirit." (Luke 23:46)
"It is finished." (John 19:30)

Meditations: Jesus on the Cross

6. The Scene of the Crime

7. The Agony of Defeat

8. The Ecstasy of Victory

9. The Letters of Paul

"The mystery of love is greater than the mystery of death"

Oscar Wilde

James F. La Croce

Author's Alert

The Gospel contradictions about "the very last words" of Jesus
remind us that the bible is a story book, not a history book,
and that bible texts cannot be used to prove anything.

No bible passages should be read personally or from the pulpit
without keeping this in mind.

Failing to do so accounts for Christianity being a house divided
and for being engaged in wars it has dared to call holy wars –
Catholics against Protestants, Christians against Muslims -
all in the name of having "the truth" about the incomprehensible
mystery of how God goes about being God on planet earth –
as Father or Mother to all born in the image and likeness of the
creator.

6. MEDITATION

The Scene of the Crime

Crucifixion was murder most foul.
Crucifixion was Rome's punishment for insurrectionists.
The crime committed was usually posted above the head.

Crucifixes were often planted along the main roads.
Crucifixes were Caesar's billboards:
"This land is my land and don't you forget it!"

Crucifixion was the most dreadful of all tortures.
The intent was to prolong this pain as long as possible.
Asphyxiation, not loss of blood, was the cause of death.

There was no significant shedding of blood.
This was not the quick and easy death of the temple lambs.
Jesus did not die as the Lamb of God.

A Mel Gibson movie, "The Passion of the Christ,"
re-enacted the crucifixion of Jesus.
Watching it made me tremble, tremble, tremble.
It was as if I were there when they crucified my Lord.

But at the end of the movie I was shocked.
I could hardly believe what I saw and heard.
Almost everyone in the theater stood up and applauded.

Jesus did this to save us from hell
was proclaimed with every clap of the hands.
Thus the standing ovation rather than an audience in tears.

How self-centered we have become.
How frightened of hell we have become.

Who can explain this, who can tell us why?

Meditation Prompt

"Dear ones beware,
beware of tiny gods frightened men
worship."

Hafiz

7. MEDITATION

The Agony of Defeat
Jesus' very last words according to Mark and Matthew

"My God, my God, why have you forsaken me?"
(Mark 15:34 and Matthew 27:46)

My
God
my
God
my
God

why have you-----forsaken me?

Why
why
why
why
why
why
why
why
why
why?

Meditation Prompt

"You would have expected Jesus
to cry out:
'Amen! My life for the world's future!' "

G.B. Shaw

"In murderous times the heart
breaks and breaks and lives
by the breaking."

Stanley Kunitz

These
are
not
the
very
last
words

of the son of God whose---------crowned and crucified body

paid
Satan's
ransom
and
satisfied
God's
wrath
and
saved
Christians
from
the
fires
of
hell

Meditation Prompt

"How did it happen that Christians
wished to see their God suffer and die?
Who released this gushing spring?
Who had thus struck the church in its very heart?"

Emile Male

These
are
the
very
last
words

of a man of God ------- on a mission from God
but
felt
abandoned
by
the
very
God
who
gave
him
this
mission

Meditation Prompt

An operatic death

"My own tears abandoned me."

Donizetti

"I would rather die than dance again."

Puccini

8. MEDITATION

The Ecstasy of Victory
Jesus' very last words according to Luke and John

"Father, into thy hands I commend my spirit." (Luke 23:46)
"It is finished." (John 19:30)

F
a
t
h
e
r

Into thy hands I commend my spirit

i
t

i
s

f
i
n
i
s
h
e
d

Meditation Prompt

A Messianic Death

"As in Adam all die, so also in Christ
shall all be made alive."

(1 Corinthians 15:22)

"For God so loved the world that he gave his only son,
so that everyone who believes in him may not perish
but may have eternal life." (John 3:16)

(These often-cited quotes lift up Christ but put down most of
humanity. John 3:16 is often seen displayed at football games and on
billboards.)

9. MEDITATION

The Letters of Paul
(Written decades before the Gospels)

Months before his birth
Mary predicted her son
would be the lion of God.
He would put down the mighty
and lift up the lowly.

Decades after his crucifixion
Paul proclaimed her son died as the lamb of God.
His blood satisfied divine wrath and paid Satan's ransom
but only for those who believe in Jesus Christ crucified.

In Paul's mythological wars
between God's wrath against all his children,
between almighty God and a mighty Satan,
both agreed, as all do in war:
There will be blood! There will be hell to pay!

Meditation Prompt

Belief in the crucifixion as a victory has a dark side.
No father has ever been so cruel to his son,
nor denied love to so many of his children.

No religion has ever been so heavily laden with fear.

P.S. The belief that there is no hell does not mean there is no heaven, not if God is infinite love and especially since, for so many of God's images and likenesses, life is a bitch and then it ends.

Pardon the Interruption

An Easy Essay

"...by the cross we mean ...the central moment in a divine event which only the Church remembers and the continuing meaning of which only the Church can know." John Knox

If Christians believe the Israelite Community of God the Father wrongly remembered the divine event of the Messiah, then they should also believe that the Christian Community of God the Son can wrongly remember the divine event of the Crucifixion.

Surely both events were gracefully remembered when experienced by each community. Just as surely they were remembered within the limits of their primitive and patriarchal cultures.

The land of milk and honey, promised and delivered, is now a land of war and terror. Jesus' prayer for a kingdom on earth is still a prayer unanswered.

Not so, say traditional Christian teachers. The kingdom on earth is a spiritual kingdom. It is the community of true believers.
It is the community of those who put their faith in Jesus Christ crucified and risen. Whether this community is the Catholic or Protestant church is still being debated. Neither Church seems to fit the description of the kingdom of God on earth.

Not to worry, say other traditional Christian teachers.
The earthly kingdom will come when Jesus returns at the end of history. He will return as the Nazarene maddened with rage.
He will lead an army in an apocalyptic fury that would be the envy of Hitler and Stalin. He will atone for having preached that God's kingdom will come without violence.

This apocalyptic ending to the Jesus story is more than a problem.
It is a travesty to the Jesus portrayed in the Gospels.
It blasphemes the name of God as Father.
It promotes the belief that Love cannot be the final solution, not even infinite love.

What a sorry ass grace the kingdom of God would be
if it came wrapped in the wrath of God.

This wrath tradition gives life to a suspect proverb:
"Religion is for those who are afraid of going to hell.
Spirituality is for those who have been there."

(author unknown to me)

Meditation Prompt for chapter two

The very last words of Jesus on the cross?

"My God, my God, why have you forsaken me?"
"Father, into thy hands I commend my spirit."

Clearly the bible is not a book of proofs.
Neither text can be claimed to be Jesus' very last words.

But both texts raise questions about Christian Tradition:
If Jesus died in the agony of defeat, belief in him as Savior is suspect.
If Jesus died in the ecstasy of victory, it was victory only for the few.

Chapter Three
Looking at the Cross, what do I see?

"What stays with you the latest and the deepest,
of curious panics,
of hard fought engagements,
or sieges tremendous,
what deepest remains?"

Walt Whitman
"The Wound Dresser"

Meditations: Looking at the Cross I see

10. The Crib
11. The Mother
12. The Brothers
13. The Beloved Disciple

14. The Third Thief
15. The Third Mount

16. The Sign on the Cross
17. The Sign of the Cross
18. The Fantasy Cross
19. The True Cross

20. The Cross on the Altar
21. The Cross of Constantine
22. The Cross and the Cloisters
23. The Cross and the Cathedral

24. The Cross and the Facts
25. The Cross and the Foot Ritual

26. The Cross in the East
27. The Cross and the Bo Tree
28. The Cross and the Kingdom Tree

29.The Cross and the Avatar

30. The Man on the Cross

Meditation Prompt

"We cannot ponder life for long
without searching for the possibilities
within death.

This may be the only obsession
which is worth its weight upon the heart."

Emily Dickinson

10. MEDITATION

The Crib

In the crib and cross stories
Jesus is the revelation of God,
unlike any god or goddess story ever told.

With the wood of the crib and of the cross,
Jesus takes the image of God as almighty presence
and beats the hell out of it.

The infant Jesus and the crucified Jesus,
gurgling in the crib and agonizing on the cross,
reveal how God goes about being God on planet earth.

This is not an almighty male God we see before us,
the touchy-tetchy Lord who flooded the world,
the Lord who can't stand the stench of sin.

The crib and cross stories reveal divine love without wrath.
They tell us in no uncertain terms:
"There is nothing to fear but fear itself."

Meditation Prompt

"From all eternity
God lives on a maternity bed.
The essence of God is birthing."

Meister Eckhart

11. MEDITATION

The Mother

My body magnified the Lord
the day I conceived a son,
as promised by Abraham to Israel.

I did not revere my son as the son of God.
He was my son.
I did not adore him as I nursed, wiped and washed him.
I made a man out of him, from breast to Bar Mitzvah.

He was not born to be crucified.
I did not raise him to be taken to the woodshed on your behalf.
I raised him to be the lion not the Lamb of God.
He was sent by God to lift up the lowly and put down the mighty.
No more crumbs from the Father's table for the poor.
No more "lording" by the mighty.
The rich, whose gold is fools' gold, will be sent away empty.

If you love my son take up his cross and follow him.
Try to treat the least as he did: do it for his sake.
Those who lose their life for his sake will gain it.

Carrying the least on his back
was just as hard for him as it will be for you.

As for me, I was no Madonna.
I was a slightly overweight Jewish peasant woman.
I enjoyed a glass of wine, good wine, as much as anyone in Nazareth.
I loved to go to weddings where the wine was the best available.

There are some tall tales told about a virgin conception.
None were told by me or my son.

Meditation Prompt

"I am
a hole in a flute
that the Christ breath moves through -
listen to this
music."

Hafiz

12. MEDITATION

The Brothers

Brother against brother
was the first sin
after the very first sin.

The smoke of Abel's animal sacrifice went up.
The smoke of Cain's grain sacrifice went down.
In his anger Cain could not kill God so he killed Abel.

It was murder most foul, committed over religious rituals.
The sin of Cain rears its ugly head even in the best of families,
as noted in the reference to Jesus' brothers in John 7: 3-5.

In that Gospel story Jesus does not want to go to Jerusalem.
Some of his enemies are plotting to kill him there.
His brothers, surely aware of this danger, nevertheless taunt him:

"No one who wants to be widely known acts in secret...
Go to Judea so your disciples there may see the works you are doing."

His brothers taunted him but did not go with him.
Not one brother comforted him at his crucifixion.

In this story it was the brothers of Jesus not "the Jews"
who bore the mark of Cain.

Meditation Prompt

In the book "Legends of the Bible" Cain pleads, "Not Guilty".
His defense was that he had never seen a man killed:
"How was I to know that the stones I threw would kill my brother?"

Can Christianity continue to so plead in self defense?
How were we to know that our doctrines
would kill your kingdom on earth mission?

13. MEDITATION

The Beloved Disciple

In John's memories, dreams and reflections,
the man on the cross was more God than Galilean.
He was the word of God and the word was God.

His song was not Mary's song.
In it Jesus is in a "word" not in a "womb."
The Word became flesh
and lived among us,
only to show his power and his glory,
the glory of the Father's only Son.

To those who believed in him, and only to them,
he gave the power to become the sons of God.

He came not to put down the mighty and lift up the lowly,
but to bear witness to the power and glory of God.

Author's Note:

Mary may or may not have sung the song attributed to her.
The apostle John did not write the Gospel attributed to him.

Gospel Mary could never have sung John's song.
Nor could Gospel John have sung Mary's song.
Their experiences of Jesus would not allow it.

My religious experience of Jesus favors Mary's song.
That of most Christians favors the song of John.

Biblical texts can only be cited to make a point not to prove a point.

Not keeping this in mind explains why Christianity is a house divided.

Still, the significance of Mary's description compared to John's cannot be denied. Her song rightly predicted how Jesus would go about his business in Galilee, as a Galilean ministering to the wretched.

Meditation Prompt

"Many a long dispute among Divines may be thus abridged;
It is not so. It is so. It is not so."

(Author unknown to me)

14. MEDITATION

The Third Thief

Jesus was crucified between two thieves.
One of them mocked him:
Hey, Savior, can't ya even save yourself?
He made no response.

The other thief pleaded like a pious Protestant:
Lord, remember me when you enter your kingdom.
Jesus responded in kind:
This day you will be with me in Paradise.

The thief who stole heaven is a story told only by Luke.
It is a "Mission Accomplished" story.
There is no place in it for the godforsaken cry of Jesus:
My God, my God, why have you forsaken me?

When I look at the cross what do I see?
I see the cross that mugged Jesus.
The cross is the third thief.
Calvary is the scene of the crime.

When I look at the man who was mugged what do I hear?
I could have ministered to a ripe old age,
I could have restored Paradise in Galilee,
I could have been Beowulf before there was Beowulf.
I could have been Beowulf without the war gear.
My God, my God, why have you forsaken me?

Meditation Prompt

Beowulf, a Scandinavian hero
who encounters the monster,

defeats it, and then lives in the exhausted aftermath.

A tall tale with immense emotional credibility.

15. MEDITATION

The Third Mount

On Mount Olympus
gods and goddesses made nuisances of themselves
with their power plays.

On Mount Sinai
the God of Israel revealed himself
as the one and only almighty power player.

Mountain gods
are to be adored, feared, worshiped,
and placated.

But on Mount Calvary
a unique incarnation of God
betrays these traditions.

Is this how he expects to get the god-job done?
Where's the testosterone?
Is this a lesser God I see before me?

Was he serious in his sermon on the Mount?
Will we inherit the earth if we are meek?
Are we to turn the other cheek as he did?

Meditation Prompt

"You are the salt of the earth;
but if the salt loses its strength,
what shall it be salted with?
It is no longer of any use
but to be thrown out

and trodden underfoot by men."

(Matthew 5:13)

16. MEDITATION

The Sign on the Cross
Pilate: "INRI"
(Latin acronym for Jesus of Nazareth, King of the Jews)

Pontius Pilate, Procurator of Judea,
Vicar of the wrath of Caesar,
angered by the Palm Sunday Procession,
kept a close watch on Jesus.

When a mob turned against Jesus
and he cried out "No sword play"
and his apostles fled in fear,
Pilate could not have been more pleased.

Clearly Jesus was a wimp.
His apostles were no better.
This was a band of wimps led by a wimp.
How foolish he was to be concerned.

Pilate could not have been more relieved.
This Jew was no Moses or David.
What belonged to Caesar would remain with Caesar.
He could arrest and crucify Jesus without losing a man.

The kingdom on earth would not begin in Caesar's Galilee.
Pilate was on top of his game.
His INRI nailed above the head of Jesus
was his sign of Roman contempt.

Meditation Prompt

"…no matter what God's power may be, the first aspect of God is never that of absolute master, the almighty. It is that of God who puts himself on our human level and limits himself."

Jacques Ellul

17. MEDITATION

The Sign of the Cross
Paul: "Christ Crucified"

Paul took no note of Pilate's sign on the cross.
He saw only the body of Christ on the cross.
Not the body of the missionary Jesus,
but the body of the risen Christ.

Paul saw the cross
in the light of the resurrection,
not the ministry of Jesus,
not his parable of the Judgment of the Nations.

Paul took no note of the Adam story
as a Paradise on earth story,
Paradise lost in Iraq,
Paradise to be regained in Galilee.

Paul did take note of the Adam Story.
as a story that put down humanity to lift up Jesus,
a story that became a theology in Romans 5:18:
Through one man sin,
through one man redemption

With this theology in hand,
the agony of a devastating and humiliating defeat
was turned into the ecstasy of a glorious victory -
but only for those who believed in Jesus.

Meditation Prompt

Paul was unable to concede
what Christians still refuse to proclaim:

God's love is not a love wrapped in wrath,
a wrath that condemned all humanity,
that demanded: "There will be blood!"

18. MEDITATION

The Fantasy Cross

"No one comes to the Father except through me."
(John. 14:6)

When I look at the cross on the Steeple,
what do I see?
I see a crucifix without a body.
I see a cross that looks like a key.
In fantasy land it is the key only for the Elect.

Beneath the steeple cross
I see a venerated house of worship,
the best the Community can build,
for that is where the faithful gather,
where they ritualize their great expectations.

Synagogues, Mosques and Temples
are not blessed with the sign of the cross.
Jews, Muslims and Indians from India
worship God without the assurance of "the cross."
Their expectations are suspect.

In a world becoming one world,
by reason of the marvels of mass communication,
not by the grace of Christian baptism
the cross on the steeples
has become a sign of perdition not benediction.

It is a fantasy Christianity can no longer afford.

Meditation Prompt

"If one knew…the facts, would one
have to feel pity even for the planets?
If one reached what they called
the heart of the matter?"

Graham Greene

19. MEDITATION

The True Cross

"If any want to become my followers let them deny themselves
and take up their cross and follow me."

(Mk. 8:34; Mt. 16:24; Lk. 9:21)

When I look at the Steeple,
hearing the peal of those words,

I ask myself:
what is the cross Jesus commanded me to carry?

It is not the cross of bearing patiently with my tribulations.
Everyone carries that cross no matter their faith.

It is not the cross of living a decent and honest life.
All believers carry this cross no matter their faith.

It is not the cross of living a Christian life.
Christianity is a house divided on what this is.

It must be the cross he himself carried,
the cross of treating the least as he treated them.

This cross has not been carried by faint-hearted followers of Jesus.
That's me, and most likely you.

Not even Jesus' madder than hell parable
has moved me to take up HIS cross and follow him.

Meditation Prompt

While pondering, keep this in mind:
Meditation is non-judgmental by nature,
always probing, never commanding,
hard-wired against feelings of guilt,
and is at its best when
stripped of our illusions and pretensions.

James F. La Croce

20. MEDITATION

The Cross on the Altar

"This is my body....this is my blood"

With these words, Catholic tradition tells us,
the Passover table became the Christian altar.

Jesus died at the altar-table before he died on the cross,
a ritual for remembering/re-enacting our Redemption.

The back stories of this most sacred tradition:
Jesus' divinity, God's holy wrath, Satan's unholy demands.

AND YET

In the Roman Catholic Mass today,
the table is preferred over the altar.

We take the bread as our spiritual food,
standing and singing and celebrating the grace of community.

We are the body of Jesus,
we are his kingdom on earth missionaries.

We no longer eat this bread as the Elect;
as if it saves us and condemns all others.

Meditation Prompt

Our mothers, unlike the mother of James and John,
should no longer be preoccupied as to where we will be seated in
heaven.

It is time to profess in our creeds:
Jesus set his Passover table to feed those who feed the wretched.

It is time to ask whether we are guilty of selfish love:
"Some people, I swear, want to love God
in the same way they love a cow.
They love it for its milk and cheese and beef
and the profit they will derive from it."

Source unknown to me

21. MEDITATION

The Cross of Constantine

"Conquer by this"

He saw a cross of light in heaven,
a marvel of grace reversing itself;
the Jesus who would rather be the nail
now preferred to be the hammer.

Constantine's vision
delivered a military victory
with the twin weapons of cross and sword,
one to capture the soul, the other the body.

What followed was a frenzy to build churches,
a luxury which had been unimaginable.
No money was spared in making expensive bibles.
The parchment alone cost the hide of about 5,000 cows.

The Jesus movement in Galilee
became Christianity in Constantinople.
And this dramatic reincarnation
is now the religion we love and live by.

The Sermon on the Mount in Galilee,
so eloquently preached by the Nazarene,
gave way to the sermon on the Mount in Hollywood,
so bluntly proclaimed by John Wayne:

"I won't be wronged!
I won't be insulted!
I won't be laid a hand on!"
Truth be told

John Wayne's words
make my U.S.A. soul cry out "Yes!",
until I see Jesus wronged, insulted, hands laid on.

"Men never do evil so completely as when they do it with religious conviction."

Blaise Pascal

22. MEDITATION

The Cross and the Cloisters

"A Silent Rebellion" A.M. Allchin

Empire, soldiers, clergy and citizens
were of one mind and heart
in pledging allegiance to the cross as a sword.

The kingdom parables and ministry of Jesus,
the priority he gave the wretched and the poor,
gave way to Constantine's conquering cross.

Who could argue with the wealth and splendor,
with the power and the glory,
and the pride and prejudice of Empire Christianity?

Only a few, like the Holy Family,
fearing the wrath of the king,
fled into Egypt.

This silent rebellion,
more a retreat than a rebellion,
gave Christianity the grace of monasticism.

Though the cloisters did not usher in the kingdom on earth,
they did give us Christians
willing to lose their lives for Jesus' sake.

Meditation Prompt

"If any want to become my followers.
let them deny themselves,
and take up their cross and follow me.

For those who want to save their life will lose it.
and those who lose their life for my sake will find it."
(Mt. 16: 24-25)

Read "The Monks of Tibhirine" by John W. Kiser
See the movie: "Of Gods and Men."

23. MEDITATION

The Cross and the Cathedral

Every stain in every stained-glass window,
every penny of the gazillions spent,
every drop of sweat of every laborer,
glorify God in every Cathedral ever built.

Nothing is too good for God!

Every Pope, Cardinal, and Bishop,
every Christian Prelate since Constantine,
every choir and organ master,
rightly provide us with pious pomp and royal ritual.

Nothing is too good for God's people!

And yet, my fellow Christians,
we must deal with the single-minded Galilean,
whom some would call simple-minded,
who ended his ministry to the wretched with whip in hand.

God's House has been made a den of thieves!

Meditation Prompt

(Isaiah 1: 11, 17, 18)

"What to me is the multitude of your sacrifices, says the Lord...
learn to do good, seek justice, rescue the oppressed..."
How odd of God to prefer Justice over Worship.

It takes a helluva lot of time and money to build Cathedrals.
It takes a helluva lot of time and money to rescue the oppressed.
How odd of us to prefer worship over justice.

24. MEDITATION

The Cross and the Facts

The Facts

He was a Jew of the first third of the first century.
He was born in a Roman occupied State.
He went about his business as a prophet not as a priest.

He was revered for his mighty works on behalf of the wretched.
He favored parables over doctrines and creeds.
He put nothing in writing.

He prayed and worked for the kingdom on earth.
He expected his followers to do the same.
He was a game-changer in his commitment to nonviolence.

He was caught up in the never-ending war between lowly and mighty.
He fell victim to the wrath of the mighty.
He expected his followers to take up his cross.

The Other Facts

He was caught up in mythological wars.
He was a pawn in a war between God and Satan;
He was a pawn in a war between God and his holy wrath.

He rose from the dead to glorify his power over death.
He is now with us as our ticket to eternal life.
He is no longer the Son sent to usher in the kingdom on earth.

Meditation Prompt

The facts and the other facts
should promote dialogue not division.

"… a good drama aspires to be, and a tragedy must be,
a depiction of human interaction in which both antagonists
are, arguably, in the right."

David Mamet

James F. La Croce

25. MEDITATION

The Cross and the Foot Ritual

The washing and nailing of Jesus' feet
are irretrievably enmeshed events.

At the table and on the cross
the master plays the role of the servant.

There is no lording by the Lord,
at the table and on the cross.

The prophet becomes a parable:
No more lording, not in my name.

………………..

No way say his apostles,
no lording means no authority.

You can be humble and get away with it,
but not us.

We need all the authority we can muster.
Without it there would be no community.

You can be a lord without lording,
but not us; we are not you.

Case Closed!

Meditation Prompt

"You call me Teacher and Lord-
and you are right, for that is what I am.
So if I, your Lord and Teacher, have washed your feet,
you also ought to wash one another's feet." (John 13: 12-14)

The foot ritual is still with us,
but only as a ritual,
only as an empty formality.

26. MEDITATION

The Cross in the East

"The wind of change was blowing in the East,
and, for some, it spelled only trouble."

Glen Baxter

When the Baptist predicted The Perfect Storm,
an eastern storm that would fill every valley and level every
mountain,
the crowd cried out in dismay:
"What then shall we do?"

Pulling no punches he replied:
"Whoever has two coats
must share with anyone who has none;
and whoever has food must do likewise."

The Perfect Storm rising in the East
spelled trouble for some,
but only in Galilee
not in the Greco-Roman West.

Mountains were not leveled,
valleys were not filled,
the mighty were not put down,
the lowly were not lifted up.

Nothing could be more frightening to Christianity today
than the wind of change blowing from the East,
the wind that will take it back to the Future,
to the kingdom on earth mission of Jesus.

Meditation Prompt

"Nothing seemed as scary as waking up at 40
and realizing that I had not lived a very courageous life."

Brit Marling, female Hollywood screenplay writer,
as reported by Emma Rosenblum,
New York Times Magazine article
Re: "How to Succeed Despite Being Very Beautiful."

27. MEDITATION

The Cross and the Bo Tree

Siddhartha Gautama,
meditating under the Bo or Bodhi tree,
accepted suffering as inevitable.

Jesus of Nazareth,
nailed to the tree of the cross,
accepted suffering as inevitable.

Both lamented and confronted human suffering.
The lives of both are mixtures of facts and fiction.
The fiction probes the mysteries behind the facts.

The teaching of the Buddha,
five hundred years before Jesus,
influenced more than half the human race.

The teaching of the Nazarene,
revered as the anointed one of God,
is a cornerstone of Western Civilization.

Both demanded great renunciation.
Both have had followers down through the ages.
Many of them have yet to sit under the tree or carry the cross.

Siddhartha and Jesus probed the mystery of suffering,
one doing so in the Far East,
the other in the Near East.

Meditation Prompt

"For is not the East the mother of spiritual Humanity, and does not the West, do not the children of the West, amidst their games and plays, when they get hurt, when they get famished and hungry, turn their face to the serene mother, the East?"

Rabindranath Tagore

28. MEDITATION

The Cross and the Kingdom Tree

The fruit of this Tree
will be the kingdom of God on earth,
Paradise Regained,

when each Jesus Community
takes up the cross he carried

when his ministry to the least
is the Community Cornerstone

when that most sacred of ministries
is ritually celebrated

when Christian eyes
are on the kingdom on earth.

Our Father/Mother in heaven
will have a kingdom on earth.

God's will *will* be done
On earth as it is in heaven.

Meditation Prompt

The lure of heaven and threat of hell
are for the children of a lesser god.

29. MEDITATION

The Cross and the Avatar
("Avatar" in Sanskrit: "Someone who descends")

In Hindu mythology
Vishnu descends in another form
to suffer the travails of the Hindus,
to preserve and maintain their world.

In Hollywood mythology
an ex-marine descends in another form
to suffer the travails of the Navi,
to preserve and maintain their world.

In Christian mythology
Yahweh descends in another form
to suffer our travails
but with minimal concern for our world.

WRONG!

Before being crucified
Yahweh's avatar, Jesus,
descended into table bread and wine
as food for those whose mission
is to restore and preserve his kingdom on earth.

Meditation Prompt

I/
Have/Learned/So much from God/
That I can no longer/Call/Myself
A Christian, a Hindu, a Muslim

A Buddhist, a Jew....

Hafiz

30. MEDITATION

The Man on the Cross

Q. Who was that man from Cross?
A. He was a man sent by God.

Q. Where did he come from?
A. He came from the Paradise Lost and Promised Land stories.

Q. Where did he go?
A. He went straight for the kingdom on earth story.

Q. What did he do with that mind-bending story?
A. He prayed for it in his prayer to Our Father in heaven.
A. He worked for it by treating the wretched as if they were himself.

Q. Did he do this as one of the Trinity or as one of us?
A. He did it by walking the roads of Galilee, not by walking on water.

Q. Did he expect his followers to treat the wretched as the key to this kingdom?
A. Hell, Yes.

Meditation Prompt

Reflect on Mt. 25: 31- 46, with this quip in mind:

"Why a child of four could understand this report.
Run out and find me a four year old child.
I can't make head or tail out of it."

Groucho Marx

75

Meditation Prompt for chapter three:

Looking at the cross what do I see?

"The most beautiful thing we can experience
is the mysterious. It is the source of
all true love and science."

Albert Einstein

Chapter Four
A Cross Examination

The sad game
Blame

Keep the sad game going.
It keeps stealing all your wealth -
giving it to an imbecile
with no financial skills.

Dear One,
Wise
Up.

Hafiz

Meditations: The cross-examination

31. The Siblings and the Cross

32. The Nazis and the Cross

33. The Vatican and the Cross

34. The Caper and the Cross

Pardon the Interruption

An Easy Essay

Our revelation tradition is rightly revered as sacred for those of us who ask, where did we come from and where are we going? We have learned to count on our communal religious imagination in coming to a decision. In so doing we have come to respect the imagination as the god-spot of the mind. Our communal stories have enabled us to believe in a God who cares.

But critics scoff at us:
You read the bible as if it were a book of facts. You can't get enough of the so-called eye-witness reports about what God said and did in such and such a place and at such and such a time. You refuse to admit that these books were written to advertise and promote a brand of religion. The authors should be scorned by you, not revered. The bible is the opium of the people.

But as G. B. Shaw noted, critics are to authors what pigeons are to statues. The critics in this case take no note of current scholarship. Since the time of Darwin and the science of biblical criticism the bible is studied and revered as legendary accounts of the religious experiences of two great communities. These communities are rightly revered even in today's world. Cynicism is the opium of skeptics.

Still, the revelation religions are not above criticism in a world rapidly becoming one by the miracles of communication not the grace of conversion. Planet earth can no longer tolerate the war chant of the revelation religions: "We have the truth, you do not!"

It is in this spirit that we cross-examine the Gospel story of the cross.

31. MEDITATION

The Siblings and the Cross

Mother Israel gave birth to Christianity

when Rome crucified a Jew named Jesus,
when the Gospel was preached in Galatia not Galilee,
when circumcision and kosher meals were no longer required,
when there were more Gentile than Jewish Jesus followers.

Mother Israel gave birth to Judaism

when Rome destroyed the Jerusalem Temple,
when the Synagogues kept Israel's faith alive,
when the priests gave way to the rabbis,
when the Jews were banished from Palestine.

For two thousand years
the World has yet had occasion to proclaim:
"See how those siblings love one another!"
There has never been a Judeo-Christian tradition.

The cross is the reason why this has been so,
for even in the inspired story of the Holy Gospels,
the Jews are condemned as Christ killers,
an accusation echoed down through the centuries.

Meditation Prompt

The ministry of a Jew only to Jews,
the seeds of a kingdom sown only in Jewish villages,
and the grace of Jesus' great expectations of a Jew in Galilee,
proved to be an unlucrative business. Israel's first-born,
Christianity, must bear most of the burden of grief and regret.

32. MEDITATION

The Nazis and the Cross

In his Creed, "Mein Kampf" (My Struggle),
and under the Swastika double-cross,
Adolf Hitler inaugurated his kingdom on earth.

Its creed was to kill the killers of Christ.
Its most sacred liturgy was celebrated
in furnaces in Germany and Poland,
where the fires were stoked by religious anti-Judaism,
a much more reliable fire than racial anti-Semitism.

Trains traveling by day as well as night,
transported neighbors and fellow countrymen
from the comfort of their homes straight to hell,
now located in the bosom of two Christian Nations.

Even Christian Nations like ours
did not leap quickly and passionately
in opening its arms to Jews fleeing the wrath of Hitler.
A boatload had gotten as far as the coast of Florida,
but was sent back to Hitler, children included.

Some Jews escaped the wrath of Hitler but not his creed.
They too came to believe that violence is the Final Solution.

Hitler's reign of terror was justified by a tall tale:
At the trial of Jesus
Pontius Pilate is Mr. Nice Guy.
With cruel lips and forked tongue he declares:
"I am innocent of the blood of this just man."
At that very same trial
the Jews are the bad guys:

"The Whole People said in reply:
Let his blood be on us and on our children."

This tall tale gave Hitler a leg-up as his storm troopers
goose-stepped through the ghettos of Christian Nations.

Meditation Prompt

"Such tales are to be learned upon no more than a bush
that tears from its roots and blows about in the wind."

Norman Mailer

33. MEDITATION

The Vatican and the Cross

Down through the ages the cross has been
a visible sign instituted by Christianity
to disgrace, not grace, the Jews.

After almost two thousand years
the Vatican finally proclaimed that "The Jews"
were not to be accused of and reviled as "Christ killers".

But there was no call for a public confession of sin
by the Roman Catholic Communities.

If there had been such a call, even by the Pope,
it would have been scorned by most Catholics.

This should not come as a surprise.
Confessing personal sins is a revered tradition.
But the opposite is true for Community sins.

A Community delights in celebrating the glories of the past.
But past Community sins are never repented by a Community.
That would be too demeaning.
They are best forgotten.

This is so for countries as well as churches.
God help any preacher who dares to call for a national penance,
or dares to proclaim that God may make a nation pay for its sin.
If he does dare, he better be damn careful on how he does it.

This was so even for the national sin of enslaving African Americans,
while at the very same time proclaiming that all men are created
equal.

God help any Christian who publicly judges any nation
as did Jesus in his Parable of the Judgment of the Nations.

As for the Johnny come lately Vatican admission that
"The Jews" are not to be reviled as "Christ Killers,"
the timing was anything but graceful,
being proclaimed post-Hitler rather than pre-Hitler.

Meditation Prompt

"There is a lot under the surface of life, everyone knows that.
A lot of malice and dread and guilt…and so much where you
wouldn't expect to find it either."

Marilynne Robinson

34. MEDITATION

The Caper and the Cross

A caper is a gay bounding leap,
a capricious escapade, an illegal enterprise,
surpassing normal physical and social limits.
The Caper is a recurring human fantasy.

In Greek mythology
Prometheus stole fire from the gods,
Daedalus made wings with which to fly.

In Christian lore
Jesus stole the hell fire from Satan,
ascended into heaven without wings.

The crucifixion was a caper,
if it paid Satan's ransom demand,
if God and Satan agreed: There will be blood!

The ascension of the crucified Jesus was a caper,
if the baptism he commanded
was not the baptism he received from John.

Meditation Prompt

No one is born as a prisoner of Satan,
nor as an enemy of our Father in heaven.
Our baptism and crucifixion rituals
Perpetuate this recurring human fantasy.

"The whole character of creation
was determined by the fact

that God was to become man
and dwell in the midst of creation."

Iranaeus

Meditation Prompt for chapter four:

A Cross Examination

"Anyone
who has the power
to make you believe in absurdities
has the power
to make you commit injustice.

As long as
people believe in absurdities
they will continue to commit atrocities."

Voltaire

Chapter Five
Christianity: Back to Ordinary Time

"The opposite of faith is not doubt,
but certainty. Certainty is missing
the point entirely."

Ann Lamott

Meditations: Christianity in Ordinary Time

35. The Enemy is Us

36. Baptism Betrayed

37. Lies of Silence

38. Our Touchy-Tetchy God

> "Never, never may the fruit
> be plucked from the bough
> and gathered into barrels...
> He that would eat of love
> must eat it where it lands."
>
> Edna St. Vincent Millay

Author's Alert

The only thing we can "know" for certain
about how God goes about being God
on planet earth, is "his" will to be a silent, unseen,
and barely perceptible presence. God did not
create the world in six days by simply saying
let there be this and let there be that.

35. MEDITATION

The Enemy is Us

We worship God as an almighty presence
and in so doing tell stories of His murderous schemes,
such as flooding the world and killing Egyptian babies.

We pray to God as our Father in heaven,
with no mention of hell in that prayer.
and yet backing away from hell is our primary concern.

We fear God as a Judge who goes by the book.
Our creeds and doctrines pay no attention whatsoever
to the Parable of the Prodigal Son.

We proclaim we have the truth, and nothing but the truth.
We blaspheme the incomprehensible mystery.
We condemn all other religions, with or without revelations, as
"false".

In a world becoming one by the miracles of mass communication,
not by the grace of baptism,
Christianity has been more a disgrace than a grace.

The Enemy is Us!

Meditation Prompt

"Love is never any better than the lover."

Toni Morrison

36. MEDITATION

Baptism Betrayed

Jesus was baptized with many other Jews,
a baptism of repentance for personal sins,
in preparation for the coming of the kingdom to Galilee.

The crowd asked John: "What sins are you talking about?"
John replied: "Whoever has two coats must share
with anyone who has none, and whoever has food must do likewise."

The baptism in which Jesus was baptized
was not the baptism with which nations were baptized,
a Mafia baptism, an offer they could not refuse.

In the novel "The Black Robe" an Iroquois Indian rightly refuses this
baptism:

"But my people are not baptized with the water sorcery.
Therefore they are not in your paradise. Why would I
want to go to a paradise where there are none of my people?
No, I will die and go to another country where our dead have gone.
There I will meet my wife and son. Your God shits on mine."

In the history of Christianity we have the scandal of the Baptism
Wars:

Send in the army said Constantine.
First the sword, then the baptism.
Amen to that said the Crusaders and the Conquistadors

Baptize the Indians cried the Colonists.
Take their land and save their souls.

Treat them as they treat one another.

To arms to arms the Protestants cried!
The baptism of the Papists must be stopped!
There will be blood!

Meditation Prompt

Christian baptism is isolationist and condemnatory.
It suffers from an infallibility complex.
Those so baptized have not ushered in the kingdom on earth.
Our Father's name will not be hallowed until his kingdom comes on earth.
If our baptism tradition is not a betrayal then I'm Napoleon.

37. MEDITATION

Lies of Silence

(Pardon my experiment with candor)

The "Our Father" has inspired and comforted Christians
for centuries, especially when put to music.
And yet, not a word of it is in our creeds.

This silence is a colossal lie because
Creeds are the voice of the Community.
Our community voice clearly
is not the voice of Jesus at prayer.

Jesus said his Father's name would be "hallowed"
when his kingdom comes on earth.
The kingdom on earth is not in our creeds.

He said daily bread is the heart of the matter.
There is not a word about that in our creeds.

He said that the bad things we do are not sins.
They are trespasses against each other.
Our creeds make no sense without a belief in Sin.

He took no note of Satan and Hell in his prayer.
A Christian can hardly find a creed without featuring both.
Our creeds silence the silence of Jesus.

Meditation Prompt

"In the middle of the journey of life
I found myself astray in the dark woods
where the straight road had been lost sight of."

Dante Alighieri

38. MEDITATION

A Touchy-Tetchy God

The belief that bad behavior offends God
is deeply embedded in our minds and hearts.

It is a belief that allows us to imagine
Billions of people offending God daily.

Unfortunately it is a belief that rings true
in the piety and hymns of the most pious of us:

"Tu'n around an' tu'n yo' face
Unto them sweet hills of grace
D' pow'r of sin yo' am scornin'!

Look about an' look aroun'
Fling yo' sin-pack on d' groun'
Yo' will meet wid d' Lord in d' mornin'!"

Jack London

Meditation Prompt

Only the Lord's prayer as a creed
will convince Christians that it is in
the presence of one another that we should
fling our trespass pack to the ground.

Meditation Prompt for chapter five:

Christianity: Back to Ordinary Times

"... there is often confusion,
a sudden disquiet,
lest one has after all
confessed and repented
of the wrong things in life."

Ann-Marie Mac Donald

BOOK TWO
PARADISE: OUR FATHER'S KINGDOM ON EARTH

In Jesus' day the known world,
was the Roman Empire.
His kingdom on earth mission
was not as far-fetched as it seems today.

It was no big reach
for Jesus to believe
that what Caesar could do
surely God could do.

Author's Alert

Jesus was all fired up about the kingdom on earth.
We Christians have never understood that.

We have been raised to read the Gospel stories
with our eyes on the kingdoms of heaven and hell.

If things have not been going well on planet earth
we can figure it out for ourselves.

Book Two: Paradise: Our Father's Kingdom on Earth

Chapter 6. Jesus in His Public Square

Chapter 7. Jesus in Our Public Square

Chapter 8. Christianity in Our Public Square

Chapter 9. Jesus' Public Square Parables

"The whole character of creation was determined
by the fact that God was to become man and
dwell in the midst of creation."

Iranaeus

Chapter Six: Jesus in His Public Square

The Palestinian East
as envisioned by Jesus
was like the American West
as envisioned by Louis L'Amour:

"A big country
needing big men and women
to live in it,
and where there was no place
for the frightened and the mean."

PREQUEL

The first story of the bible is about paradise lost.
The last is about paradise regained.
Both stories are driven by the wrath of God.
That is not very encouraging.

In the first story Paradise is a garden in Iraq.
It was lost because of one act of disobedience.
Women were doubly punished. They would suffer in childbirth.
And they would accept husbands as their masters.
(Obviously this story was told in primitive and patriarchal times.)

In the second story, Paradise is a strip of land between Syria and
Egypt. It is described as the land of milk and honey and is only for
Abraham's family.
God had given up by then on the family of Adam.
In this Torah story there is no life after death, no heaven or hell.

In the third story Paradise is to begin in Galilee,
the northern sector of the Promised Land.
But Galilee was in the kingdom of Caesar.
What was Jesus to do? He had no army!

His Father had no such problem.
He was a War Lord.
He took the Paradise promised the old fashioned way.
His army was stronger than that of the occupants.

The Son had renounced the sword.
The Son was the polar opposite of the Father.
But the Son was obedient to his Father's will.
Never has a son been in such a bind.

Meditations : Jesus in his Public Square

39. Bethlehem's Star

40. Cana's Wine-Maker

41. Galilee's Missionary Man

42. Nazareth's Story Teller

43. Galilee's Resurrected Missionary

44. Jerusalem's Prophet

45. Palestine's Ascending Lord

"The wind of change was blowing in from the East.
and for some it only spelled trouble."

Glen Baxter

39. MEDITATION

Bethlehem's Star

"Where is the newborn king of the Jews?"
We (kings from afar) observed his star
at its rising and have come to pay him homage."
(Mt. 2:2)

The stories of Jesus born under a star,
like those of Jesus conceived without sex,
were never told by Mary, Jesus or Joseph.

These highly revered stories
were not even told
by Mark, John or Paul.

Jesus, Paul rightly reminds us,
"...emptied himself, taking the form of a slave,
being born in human likeness." (Philip. 2: 6-7)

Jesus did not live as one born under a star.
For about thirty of his thirty-three years
he lived the life of an anonymous Jew.

The story of the virgin, the star and the kings
is rightly cherished as a Christmas story,
but with reservations.

Meditation Prompt

The stories of a conception without male sperm,
and of a birth with angels, shepherds and kings adoring,
are stories that favor the divinity of Jesus.

But the stories of a ministry with its ups and downs,
of mighty works not as great as those of Moses,
are stories that favor the humanity of Jesus.

In Christian tradition the divinity of Jesus
has always counted more than his humanity.

Is this a grace or a disgrace?

40. MEDITATION

Cana's Wine-Maker

"The water in the (Cana) story
is our dream of eternal life with God.

The wine is Jesus' dream,
God's kingdom on earth."

Shusaku Endo

Now that would be a miracle,
changing our dream to Jesus' dream.

Not so fast you may say,
Cana is a miracle story, not a dream story.

Not so fast, my fellow Christians.
Miracle wine only intoxicates.
It has not brought peace on earth,
nor good will to all.

Surely another look at this story
cannot do us any harm,
and may even move us
to a faith that is more wine than water.

Meditation Prompt

How can our faith be changed from water to wine?

"As you go, proclaim the good news;
'the kingdom of heaven has come near.
Cure the sick, raise the dead, cleanse the lepers,
cast out demons. You received without payment,
give without payment.' "

(Mt. 10:78)

41. MEDITATION

Galilee's Missionary-Man

What did he go out to see?

Crowds that kept him busy, gave him something to do?
(until it was time to be crucified)

Crowds that would be the last of the Chosen People?
(unknowing participants in the story of their own demise)

Crowds that were but Bit Players in a divine drama?
(a mythological war between God and Satan)

Crowds that he could hardly love?
(Jews destined to be his killers)

....

What did the Galileans go out to see?

A divine miracle worker?
(The miracles of Moses were even more divine.)

A prophet proclaiming a new religion?
(Not even God could tempt the Jews to change their religion.)

A rabbi with all the answers?
(Jesus raised more questions than answers.)

A preacher who raised great expectations?
(His expectations were not theirs.)

Meditation Prompt

We will never hear the words of Jesus or be touched by him
as did those Galileans of the first third of the first century.
They had a religious experience we will never have.
But not even they lived up to his great expectations.

"The great end of life is not knowledge but action."

T.H. Huxley

42. MEDITATION

Nazareth's Story-Teller

"...there is always the chance that...
a book of fiction may throw some light
on what has been written as fact."

Ernest Hemingway

Yes, yes, Jesus says earnestly,
but there is more than a chance.
I know, I was raised on a book of stories.

If facts were crucial to my mission
I would have put everything in writing,
every word and deed, all facts and no stories.

It is no small matter
that stories about me
feature stories told by me.

Nor is it by accident
that the stories told by me
feature me favoring the poor and the wretched.

But the light shed by these stories
is hid under the bushel of other stories,
tall tales about God speaking only through males.

Surely this silly and sinister presumption
only proves that even our sacred stories
reflect the not-so-pious presumptions
of a patriarchal, pre-modern world.

James F. La Croce

Meditation Prompt

The Bible stories have been abused with impunity,
by biblical literalists who cite it as a book of proofs,
by homophobic Christians who cannot cite Jesus condemning
homosexuality,
by all Christians who cannot imagine God as a woman.

43. MEDITATION

Galilee's Resurrected Missionary

"But go, tell his disciples and Peter
that he is going ahead of you to Galilee;
there you will see him, just as he told you."

(Mk. 16:7)

Remember The Easter Proclamation :

Get thee to Galilee!
Jesus died in Jerusalem
but he left his heart in Galilee.
There you will see him as predicted,
being what he loved to be,
a saving presence to the wretched and the poor.

Tall tales will be told about an empty tomb,
stories about an Easter Parade in Jerusalem,
Easter stories children like to hear.
Blessed are they who put away the things of children.
Blessed are they who do not see and yet believe.
Blessed are they who celebrate Easter in Galilee.

Meditation Prompts

Some say that if the Apostles had a good psychiatrist
to help them deal with the crucifixion there would be no Christianity.
I am not one of them. But with the risen Jesus I do say
that believing is better than seeing and that seeing Jesus
in the least is more graceful that all the graces of all our Easter
Sundays.

" 'Christ is risen!' said Matriena Pavlovna,
leaning her head forward and smiling.
By the intonation of her voice she seemed to say,
'All are equal to-day.' "

Tolstoy

44. MEDITATION

Jerusalem's Prophet

"Lord, is this the time when you will restore the kingdom of Israel?"
(Acts 1:6)

Forty days and nights
between resurrection and ascension,

hearing the groans of the Galileans,
seeing the weakness of the Twelve,

to leave or not to leave,
that is Jesus' question.

Don't go urged the Twelve,
stroking themselves to ease their pain.

Not to worry said the Lord,
I am sending the Holy Spirit.

Yea, ok, sure, but at least tell us this, they said:
"Are you going to restore the rule of Israel now?"

"Restoring the kingdom is the right idea," he said,
"But why by me, why not by you?"

Meditation Prompt

Jesus' question "why not by you" was not part of the story in
Acts 1:6 ff.
But the Jerusalem community took shape as if it were.

"And all that believed were together,
and had all things in common;
and sold their possessions and goods,
and parted them to all men,
as every man had need."

(Acts 2: 44-45)

45. MEDITATION

Palestine's Ascending Lord

Ascension Stories Galore!

(Mt. 28: 16-20; Mk. 16: 15-20; Lk. 24: 50-53; Acts 1:9-11)

Readers Beware!

Mark: Jesus ascended from Jerusalem;
Matthew and Acts: No, it was from Galilee;
Luke: Wrong! He went to heaven from Bethany.

Critics Beware!

If the bible did not have contradictions in its stories
it would not be the bible.
Get over it!

Fellow Christians Beware!

In the ascension story Jesus' command to baptize all Nations
should be seen in light of his own baptism,
not our Christian Baptism.

Meditation Prompt

The question raised at Jesus' baptism by John:
"What shall we do to avoid God's wrath?"

The answer given by John:
"Whoever has two coats must share
with anyone who has none;

and whoever has food must do likewise."
(Luke 3:11)

Surely, the baptism command in the ascension story
should, or at least could, be seen in light of the story of Jesus' baptism
and in light of his last parable of the Judgment of the Nations,
not in light of Christian baptism and surely
nor in light of the parable of Adam's sin,
a parable never told by Jesus.

Meditation Prompt for chapter six:

Jesus in His Public Square

"He went where he was supposed to go.
He stayed where he was needed.
He took little or nothing along,
a pair of sandals, a bit of shirt,
a few odds and ends to stave off loneliness.

He never rejected the world.
If he had rejected it,
he would have been rejecting the mystery.
And if he rejected the mystery,
he would have been rejecting faith."

Colum McCann

Author's Alert

"We cannot know just how far Jesus' ideas
and his career as a whole were determined
by the political circumstances of his times,
but we can be sure the extent of this influence
is greater than the Gospels imply."

John Knox

Chapter Seven: Jesus in Our Public Square

"Let your own discretion be your tutor,
suit the action to the word, the word to the action,
with this special observance,
that you o'erstep not the modesty of nature."

Shakespeare

James F. La Croce

Meditations: Jesus in Our Public Square

46. Jesus and Jefferson

47. Jesus and Lincoln

48. Jesus and Locke

49. Jesus and Mary

"God's purpose for man
is to acquire a seeing eye
and an understanding heart."

Rumi

46. MEDITATION

Jesus and Jefferson
(Religion and Politics)

Jefferson,
more political than Jesus,
promoted new ways of distributing power,
new ideas of representation.

Jesus,
more to the heart of the matter,
proclaimed new ways of treating the least,
no matter how society is organized.

Jefferson,
a man of his time,
revered Jesus as a man,
a man after his own heart.

Jesus,
a man for all times,
and more than a man,
was for the people and of the people.

Jefferson,
in a seemingly unbecoming way
cut out the Gospel passages on Jesus' divinity,
pasting together those on his down to earth goodness.

Jesus,
in a seemingly unbecoming way
threatened with hell
all nations that did not treat the least as he did.

Meditation Prompt

Jefferson may have imagined a wall
separating Church and State but surely
never a wall between Jesus and men of State.

The Jesus Jefferson loved is the Jesus that Jesus loved.

Author's Alert

At age 77 Jefferson began to cut texts out of the Gospels,
removing passages he thought reflected the actual teaching
of Jesus and pasting them into a slim New Testament,
leaving out what he felt were the "misconceptions" of
Jesus' followers, thus "expressing unintelligibly for others
what they had not understood themselves."
(Andrew Sullivan, "Christianity in Crisis", Newsweek 4/2/12)

Our beloved president's criticism is not without foundation,
given the passages in which Jesus complains about them,
as in Mark 8: 17-18: "Do you still not perceive or understand?
Are your hearts hardened? Do you have eyes, and fail to see?
Do you have ears and fail to hear?"

If those who were taught by Jesus himself did not always understand
what he taught, then surely the Gospel writers, who were not
Matthew, Mark, Luke and John, worked within the same limitations.

As daring and dangerous as this may sound, Christian Churches
have in effect been doing what Jefferson did, not with scissors,
but by citing only those passages which suited their traditions -
thus accounting for Christianity as a house divided.

When I was in my seventies I began to do what Jefferson did.
I was not so bold as to use scissors but I feasted on those
passages which graced my life in Jesus and led to this book
of uncommon meditations.

47. MEDITATION

Jesus and Lincoln
(Leadership and Prudence)

Jesus was a prudent prophet;
When asked about Caesar he said:
Render to Caesar what belongs to Caesar.

Lincoln was a prudent president;
When asked about slavery he said:
Render to the Slave Sates what belongs to the Slave States.

Prudence, however, did not play its part.
It did not disarm the wrath of Pilate.
It did not temper the temper of the Slave States.

Prudence did not stop the crucifixion.
Prudence did not stop the assassination.
Prudence fails where sordid passions prevail.

Meditation Prompt

"Were you to put words to this
we would not survive the song."

Rumi

48. MEDITATION

Jesus and Locke
(Christianity and Capitalism)

Jesus: The main purpose of Government is to protect
the wretched, the poor, the huddled masses,
to treat them as if they were me.

Locke: The main purpose of Government is to protect
the right of the individual to acquire unlimited
amounts of property, by whatever legal means possible.

Jesus: Be a good Samaritan.
Give a helping hand to the guy or gal in the ditch.
Don't be a jerk!

Locke: Money towards charity is a waste.
It is money that could be put to better use.
Don't be a fool!

Jesus: Sharing our Father's bread
makes us a family,
and thus contributes to the common good.

Locke: Amassing property produces jobs,
provides consumer goods,
and thus contributes to the common good.

Meditation Prompt

Our political life is grounded more on Locke than on Jesus. It is more like that of the fictional "Studs Lonegan."

"Politics is a game you got to play, and you got to get what you can out of it. If you don't, you're a chump."

James T. Farrell

49. MEDITATION

Jesus and Mary
(The mighty and the lowly)

In the last story of the Hebrew Bible
a woman named Hadassah,
highly revered in the Persian Court as Esther,
saves her captive people from a cruel fate.

In the first story of the Holy Gospels
a woman named Mary,
lowly placed in Roman occupied Galilee,
predicts her son will put down the mighty.

The Jewish feast of Purim
celebrates Esther's grace-filled victory,
and celebrates it with gusto.
Rude noises are made whenever the villain's name is mentioned.

The Catholic "Hail Mary"
takes no note of Mary's grace-filled prediction,
but only asks her prayers for our sakes,
now and at the hour of our death.

Meditation Prompt

The sound of my "Hail Mary"
has been that of a small and shallow spirit,
pleading for her protection against the rudeness of death.

I would have done better to hail Mary
by making rude noises whenever the names of villains are mentioned.

Meditation Prompts for chapter seven:

Jesus in our Public Square

Our Public Square

"A nation, like a person,
has a body which must be housed and fed and clad,
and a mind which must be educated and informed,
but it also has something deeper, something more permanent,
something larger than the sum of its parts...
the spirit, the faith of America."

President Franklin Delano Roosevelt

Our Jesus

"If you are going to be involved
in seemingly futile undertakings
you might as well do it
with someone you love."

Frida Berrigan

Chapter Eight: Christianity in our Public Square

"And Jesus came and said to them (the eleven disciples),

'All authority in heaven and on earth has been given to me.
Go therefore and make disciples of all nations, baptizing them
in the name of the Father and the Son and the Holy Spirit,
and teaching them to obey everything I have commanded you.
And remember, I am with you always, to the end of the age.' "

(Matthew 28: 18-20)

Author's Alert

Some Christians however agree with
Saint Francis of Assisi:

"So precious is a person's faith in God,
so precious;
never should we harm that
because He gave birth to all religions."

Meditations: Christians in our Public Square

Traditional Christians are amply fortified
by the following key players in the Public Square.

Meditations

50. The Genesis Creator

51. The Two Stone Tablets

52. The God Book

53. The Almighty White Guy

54. The War Lord

55. The Apocalyptic Son

56. The Enshrined Mother

57. The Star Spangled Church

58. The Star Spangled Country

59. The American Mall

60. The American Political Will

James F. La Croce

"One clear pattern in history
is that where there is chaos
there is ambiguity and where
there is ambiguity there is fear,
and fear gets manipulated."

Robert Redford

50. MEDITATION

The Genesis Creator

"And on the seventh day God finished the work that he had done,
and he rested on the seventh day from all the work that he had done."
(Genesis 2: 2)

Yesterday, the creation story was taken literally.
God made planet earth as advertised,
made it in six days,
simply saying, let there be this and that.

In the very first story of the bible
the creator makes it perfectly clear,
by his instant and mighty deeds
that the Public Square belongs to Him.

"Nature and Nature's laws lay hid in the night;
God said, 'Let Newton be!' and all was light."
Alexander Pope

Today, many read Genesis in light of the sciences.
God was behind creation,
but so far behind
that this almighty presence
is barely perceptible.

Since the days of Darwin and Newton
and the flourishing of the Sciences,
it has been perfectly clear
that the public square belongs to the creatures.

Meditation Prompt

The Great Ambiguity:
Creation by fiat, an act of almighty power?
Creation by incarnation, an act of infinite love?

The Great Decision:
Revere the cosmos as the first incarnation of God,
as the revelation that even for God self-love is not enough.

The Great Confession
The words "creator" and "creature" do not
do justice to the incomprehensible mystery
we have rudely and crudely named "God".

51. MEDITATION

The Two Stone Tablets

"Moses convened all Israel, and said to them:
'Hear O Israel, the statutes and ordinances
I am addressing to you today.'"
(Deuteronomy 5:1)

Worship your God, honor your parents;
No murder, adultery, or stealing,
No false witness or coveting.

These commandments God gave to Moses,
Commands carved in stone,
were already known by all people everywhere.

Why the shaking mountain?
Why punish the children of sinners?
Why down to the third and fourth generations?
(Ex. 20:5)

Why were these commands written in stone?
Why the ironic threat of death by stoning?
Why all the melodrama?

Meditation Prompt

This stone tablet story sanctifies and solidifies
a long revered biblical tradition:
Words fly away but writing remains;
"It is written" has long been a sacred mantra.

But this biblical tradition meant nothing to Jesus.

He put nothing in writing, not one word.
His words were seeds that would bear different fruit
in different times and places, not words written in stone.

52. MEDITATION

The God Book

The God Book Yesterday

This book contains
the mind of God,
the state of man,
the way of salvation,
the doom of sinners.

It is rightly used as
the Christian's staff,
the Church's compass.
Christianity's charter,
the word of God.

The God Book Today

This book contains
a library of books,
story books about God,
stories told in primitive times,
and in a patriarchal culture.

It has long been abused
as a book of proofs,
and is most unhelpful

in proclaiming God as an almighty presence,
a God who speaks only through males.

Meditation Prompt

The God Book, though primitive and patriarchal
in its style, was conceived in the passion
of a People yearning to be free, a passion that
characterized the ministry of Jesus in Galilee.

The God Book should be read and revered
in light of these passions.

53. MEDITATION

The Almighty White Guy

" 'When Abram was ninety years old,
the Lord appeared to him and said,
'I am God the almighty.
Walk in my presence and be blameless.' "

(Genesis 17:1)

My Children beware!
I brought you into this world
And I can take you out.

My power is terrible to behold!
No reign of terror
can top me in terrorism.

Read my book!
In the beginning I flood the world,
and in the end I will destroy it with fire.

It is rightly said
that the beginning of wisdom
is fear of the Lord.

Pay heed to your creed,
revere God as the Father,
but as the Father Almighty.

Tremble, tremble, tremble,
in the almighty presence
of the architect and CEO of hell.

Meditation Prompt

Is this holy terror the God I am doomed to love?
I can fear him but cannot love him.

Only a god with a poor self- image
could be so touchy and tetchy, so easily offended.

Only a lesser god would rule by a book of laws.
Whether it be the Jewish, Christian or Muslim book is still debated.

What a sorry-ass god
for an enlightened people in an enlightened world.

54. MEDITATION

The War Lord

"After the death of Joshua the Israelites consulted the Lord,
asking, 'Who shall be first to attack the Canaanites and do
battle with them?' The Lord answered, 'Judah shall attack:
I have delivered the land into his power'."

(Judges 1: 1-2)

Israel had no regular army.
Her army was rallied
by the sound of Yahweh's trumpet.

Victories in battle belonged to God,
and sometimes the number of warriors was limited
to make this belief perfectly clear.

The War Lord could be savage beyond belief.
At his command whole populations were destroyed,
including women and children.
(Deut. 3:6-7; 20:14;
Joshua 8: 25-27)

In Israel today,
still not the land of milk and honey,
the Lord is still the War Lord.

No special shame here,
since all people protect themselves by the sword
and prosper by the sword.

What else can be done, the nations lament?
This lament rings true to me and most likely to you,

but not to Jesus, Gandhi, Martin Luther King, and Phil Berrigan.

Meditation Prompt

We claim the New Testament Jesus as Lord,
but in this matter of war,
our Lord is the War Lord of the Old Testament.

Which will it be in this third millennium?

Pardon the Interruption

An Easy Essay

Moses led Yahweh's army in Israel's Great Escape. Constantine led Christ's army in Christianity's Great Expansion. Mohammed led Allah's army in Islam's Great Dispersion.
Jesus had no army.

Surely Jesus was tempted to raise an army. Under foreign occupation the Chosen People, even more than the Colonial Americans, yearned to be free. They, too, saw war as the only path to freedom.

Not so, said Jesus, for we are born to be servants not, soldiers. Our wars are to be waged with food, shelter, and healing all who are in need. Our defense will be to turn the other cheek. Daily bread is the key to peace on earth and good will to all. This is our Father's will. His will *will* be done. His kingdom will come on earth as it is in heaven.

No way said his followers down through the centuries. Anyone who preaches this way is confusing religion with politics. There can only be peace between wars. Every nation is taken and defended the old fashioned way. It cannot be otherwise. War is hell but that is a hell we have to live with.

Right you are, says Jesus. I predicted this in my parable of the Judgment of the Nations in Matthew: 25:31-46. If nations do not treat the least as if they were me, they are doomed to live in the hell of war. Surely you do not believe that in this parable I was referring to a hell supposedly run by Satan? If I did you would all end up in hell. I can see why you never cite that parable in your sermons on Satan's hell.

James F. La Croce

War is hell! The bravery of our warriors, taken mostly from the young and the poor, has not always been well spent. They are too often and too easily sent into harm's way. Bad music never sounds so good as when marching off to war. Stories of what they do for one another in the heat of battle would make a grown man cry. And yet money spent on caring for the wounded cannot compare to money spent on killing the enemy. Any fool can see that a Nation that wages war and lowers taxes is a nation without honor.

Many more died in stopping Hitler's armies than would have died in preventing a Hitler from coming to power. Christians cowered when he was stoking his furnaces with Jews. They forgot that to be a follower of Jesus was not for the faint-hearted. WHY do we wait until there is a war to show courage?

Our non-violent Jesus has not even come close to becoming a game-changer. It isn't his fault. He was no wimp. He was feared by Pilate and the Priests as unarmed but dangerous. He stood up to pious and political bullies. He struck at the heart of darkness. He did it without slapping a face.
He was no fool. We have been the fools.

If things have not gone well on planet earth we can figure it out for ourselves.

Let us figure it out for ourselves.

In promoting the Philippine-American War President Theodore
Roosevelt condemned "Peace at any Price" talk as "unintelligent
cowardly chatter." After this war Senator George Frisbee Hoar left
Roosevelt and the American people fuming. In a speech on
the Senate floor he argued that war can be treacherous when waged in
order that apparent good may come out of real evil.

"You have wasted 600 millions of treasure.
You have sacrificed nearly 10,000 American lives,
the flower of our youth.

You have devastated provinces. You have slain
uncounted thousands of the people you desired to benefit.

Your practical statesmanship has succeeded
in converting a people who three years ago
were ready to kiss the hem of the garment of the American
and to welcome him as liberator....into sullen and irreconcilable
enemies, possessed of a hatred which centuries
cannot eradicate."

(Citation taken from Candice Millard 's book review of "Honor in the
Dust: Theodore Roosevelt, War in the Philippines, and Rise of the
Imperial Dream" by Gregg Jones.)

Meditation Prompt

"War is always about betrayal of the young by the old, of idealists by cynics,
and of troops by politicians."

Chris Hedges

"In wartime truth is so precious that she should always be attended to by a bodyguard of lies."

Winston Churchill

"Am I going to lose my legs today or die today? That's probably one of the biggest things I miss in being a civilian, is just the sense of security you have."

Lance Corporal Brian Shearer, age twenty, Rapid City, South Dakota

"War is God's way of teaching Americans geography."

Ambrose Bierce

55. MEDITATION

The Apocalyptic Son

"Next I saw a large white throne and the One who sat on it.
The earth and the sky fled from his presence
until they could no longer be seen."

(Rev. 20:11)

The book of Revelations would have us believe that
Jesus will return as the "anti-Jesus," a terrorizing persona,
a Jesus who would be the envy of Hitler and Stalin.

In this last book of the bible
violence is revealed to be the final solution to evil,
even for the Nazarene who preached and practiced non-violence,
even for the Lord who did not believe in lording.

How can this be?
What happened to the Nazarene in heaven?
While in heaven did he see his Galilee mission as a mistake?
What kind of heaven could so change Jesus?

Is the last book in our holy bible a good book for humanity?

Meditation Prompt

A terrorist Jesus is like a fish out of water:

"First
the fish needs to say,
'Something ain't right about this
Camel ride-

And I'm
Feeling so damn
Thirsty.' "

Hafiz

56. MEDITATION

The Enshrined Mother

"Ave, Ave, Ave Maria"
(Lourdes Hymn)

Most Christians
would not agree with Augustine:
"I should not be a Christian
except for miracles."

And then again, most of us
would not agree with Jesus:
"Blessed are they who have not seen
and yet have come to believe."
(John 20:29)

We do love our Gospel miracles,
especially our Easter miracles.
No one dare cast a shadow on Easter Sunday,
not even the Jesus cited above.

We do love our Shrine miracles,
especially those performed at Lourdes.
No one dare cast a shadow on Shrine Mary.
Her son's concern for the afflicted is legendary.

There is, however, some cause for concern
when Mary is enshrined in our hearts,
more for the way she heals
than for the way she raised her first-born son.

James F. La Croce

Meditation Prompt

It is truly right and just that we presume
Mother Mary sings this song to the pilgrims at Lourdes:

"Get thee to a hospital, a homeless shelter,
a soup kitchen, an inner-city health clinic.
Only your healing power can usher in the kingdom on earth.
You are the only hope for my Son's great expectations."

57. MEDITATION

The Star Spangled Church

"...you are Peter and on this rock
I will build my church..."
(Mt. 16:18)

The glory of her saints,

the self-sacrifice of her monks,

the wisdom of her theologians and philosophers,

the sacrifices of her missionaries,

the world-wide presence that makes her truly "catholic,"

the churches, basilicas, shrines and schools that are her pride and joy,

the solace of her rituals,

the safety in her tradition of obedience,

and even some left-over
time, energy, and money
given to the poor.

This is the fullness of her grace,
a grace wrapped in obedience.

Meditation Prompts

The prophets, not the popes, are the stars of the church.

The prophets
"unmask the atheism
of ritualism and all forms of religion
that do not bear fruit
in love, justice, mercy."

It is time for us to proclaim that
"...exaggerated calls to obedience
produce a useless and inauthentic person."

Bernard Haring

58. MEDITATION

The Star Spangled Country

"…in dawn's early light…."

Francis Scott Key

Bombs bursting in air
give proof through the night
that our flag is still there.

Like the Israel of old
our nation is a nation under God,
a War Lord in the public square.

But the War Lord of Moses and David
did not send to hell sinners killed in battle,
for in those days they did not believe in hell.

Whereas our Christian War Lord
sends straight to hell
unrepentant sinners killed in battle.

In light of Christian teaching yesterday and today
war sends more sinners to hell
than Hollywood and hedonism combined.

Meditation Prompt

In our long held belief in hell and war,
and in how easy it is to be sent to hell,
and in how easily we settle for war,
we are, in the dawn's early light, a silly people.

NB. There is no mention of hell, or heaven, in the first five
books of the bible, in the stories of Abraham, Moses, David,
nor even of a heaven, but only the promise of paradise in this world.

59 MEDITATION

The American Mall
"From Sea to shining Sea"

Opulence casually displayed in our Malls
is not as sinister as it may seem to be,
even in light of world poverty.

Our Malls did not rise up out of the pits of hell
but are the products of a creative and enterprising spirit,
and the belief that God wants the best for you and me.

More importantly, in no way can world poverty
be addressed or solved by a strip-tease act
by you and by me.

Indeed, the very suggestion of so doing
is a sin of the worst kind,
a good intention that has nowhere to go.

The only response to world-wide poverty
is the promotion of our nation's political will
to put into play its core belief about the wretched.

Meditation Prompt

This is our core belief

"Give me your tired, your poor, your huddled masses yearning to be free, the wretched refuse of your teeming shore. Send these, the homeless tempest-tossed to me. I lift my lamp beside the golden door."
"Lady Liberty"

Not This

"Statistics prove that the scum of Southern Europe is dumped on the nation's door in rapacious, conscienceless, lawbreaking hordes."

"The New York Herald" (as cited by Mike Dash)
An alarmist article in the Herald reporting that among the 1,400 Italian immigrants arriving on the S.S. Belgravia, one in six was found to have given false information.

60. MEDITATION

The American Political Will

Velleitas vs. Voluntas

"Velleitas" is the Latin word
for a wishy-washy will.

In the slang of my imagination
it is the will wearing a contraceptive.

In the slang of the wild west
it is the will of one who is all hat and no gun.

"Voluntas" is the Latin word
for a highly determined will.

In the prayer of Jesus
it is the "kingdom on earth" will of the Father.

In the public square ministry of Jesus
it is the will to treat the least as he would treat himself.

In the American public square
the "Voluntas" of Jesus is a grace not yet realized.

Meditation Prompt

Our Lord was Mr. Voluntas.
Our Nation has been Mr. Velleitas.

We have avoided being embarrassed by finding a way
to proclaim that Jesus was sent to save our souls, not our planet,

that his death was a victory not a defeat.

In so doing we had,

"no choice but to insist on a resurrection
and choose one among us to drag a cross,
and then leap from it and emigrate,
but not before collecting documentary witnesses;
otherwise, we are merely walking compost,
and where is the fun in that......?"

Brian Doyle

Meditation Prompt for chapter eight:

Christians in our Public Square

"You asked for my hands
that you might use them
for your purpose.
I gave them for a moment
then withdrew them
for the work was hard.

You asked for my mouth
to speak out against
injustice.
I gave you a whisper that I
might not be accused.

You asked for my eyes
to see the pain of poverty.
I closed them for I did not
want to see.

You asked for my life
that you might work
through me.
I gave a small part that I
might not get too involved.

Lord, forgive my calculated
efforts to serve you,
only when it is convenient
for me to do so,
only in those places where
it is safe to do so,

and only with those who
make it easy to do so."

Joe Seremane, 'South Africa,' quoted by Janet Morely,
editor, Bread of Tomorrow, Christian Aid, 1992.
(re-printed in Joyce Huggett's *Learning the Language of Prayer*)

Pardon the Interruption

An Easy Essay

The Pueblo Indians believed they made the sun rise and set by practicing their religion. They were convinced their religion had a crucial role to play in the survival of their world.

The Hopi Indians lived on high plateaus to avoid war, to be close to nature. "In the U.S. the Hopi religious expression remains the sole surviving taproot of an ancient American spiritual vision." Carl A. Hammerschlag.

The conquerors of the Indians, the European Christians, believed that planet earth is little more than God's Classroom for a pass/fail test which will determine who goes to heaven and who to hell. They believed that only true-blue Christians (whoever they may be) could hope to pass.

Which belief was the more enlightened, Christian or Indian? Which will better serve our planet in this cliff-hanging, nuclear-banging millennium? Were the beliefs of the Indians more faithful to the Public Square presence of Jesus than the teaching and practice of the Christians who conquered them?

Common sense and the table set by Jesus provide the answer.

A world becoming one by the miracles of mass communication and not by the grace of conversion can no longer tolerate the Christian mantra: "No one goes to the Father except through the Son". The world today needs all Christians eating and drinking at the same table, chanting the Jesus mantra: "Treat the least as if they were me."

At his last supper Jesus set his table to feed those who would minister to the least as if they were Jesus. The ministry of those who ate at his table would make the sun rise and set on a brave new world - the kingdom of God on earth.

But all too soon "the Christians" re-set the Lord's table for their personal salvation. It was now an altar-table on which his crucifixion was ritually re-enacted or remembered. Only those nourished by this ritual could hope to escape the fires of hell. Jesus was not born to usher in God's kingdom on earth, but to satisfy God's holy wrath. He was born to be crucified.

God's kingdom on earth has not come. His will has not been done. The prelates who have proclaimed themselves the official teachers of the Church must bear the burden of the blame. The theologian with her pen and the peasant with his plow have good reason not to kiss the venerable purple.

It is in his parables that Jesus has his eye on the kingdom on earth as the prize. Christianity today needs a faith that is driven more by parables and less by prelates.

Chapter Nine: Jesus' Public Square Parables

"What marks off a parable
is that it is a story…
always thought-provoking
and often is a challenge
to decisive action."

Wilfred Harrington, O.P.

Meditations: Jesus' Public Square Parables

61. Ten Great Decisions by the Parable Man

62. The Parables of Jesus

63. The Popularity of the Parable Man

My Top Ten Parables

64. The Hidden Leaven

65. The Lost Coin

66. The Motherly Father

67. The Emotional Housekeeper

68. The Good Samaritan

69. The Pharisee and the Publican

70. The Unforgiving Servant

71. The Wicked Tenants

72. The Buried Talents

73. The Judgment of the Nations

The Parable Man was more country crier than creator of creeds,
more at home with the lowly than with the mighty, more concerned
about the helluva life in Galilee than the hell in Gehenna,
and more like the Buddha than the Christ.

61. Meditation

Ten Great Decisions by the Parable Man

To live as an anonymous Jew for most of his life.

To live frugally.

To serve God as a prophet not as a priest.

To favor the poor and the wretched.

To build nothing.

To put nothing in writing.

To do no lording.

To teach us to pray to God as our Father not as his Father.

To preach the kingdom on earth.

To rely heavily on parables.

Meditation Prompt

"O the depth of the riches and wisdom
and knowledge of God! How unsearchable
are his judgments and how inscrutable
are his ways!"

(Romans 11: 33)

62. MEDITATION

The Parables of Jesus

"The great end of life is not knowledge but action."
T.H. Huxley

The plots were simple,
the characters were few,
the images were vivid.

They were told to Galileans,
hard working people,
pious peasants but not very kosher.

The stories were a tender trap,
first the appeal to the heart,
then the demand for a change of heart.

The favored theme was the kingdom,
the kingdom of God in Galilee,
as prayed for in the Lord's Prayer.

The parables were about this world,
made no mention of God,
nor any references to heaven or hell.

The hell in Jesus' last parable
is the one created on earth by the Nations
that do not treat the least as if they were Jesus.

Jesus' parables were the stories of a trouble-maker,

a visionary with tales of great expectations,
stories told to disturb the sleep of nations.

Meditation Prompt

"Every hazard is again permitted the inquirer.
Perhaps there has never been so open a sea."

John Gardner

63. MEDITATION

The popularity of the Parable Man

"Such great crowds gathered around him
that he got into a boat and sat there,
while the crowd stood on the beach,
and he told them many things in parables…"

(Luke 13: 2-3)

The word "parable"
occurs about fifty times in the Gospels,
depending on how one is counting.

Nowhere in the New Testament
is the teaching voice of Jesus
so clearly heard as it is in the parables.

However, Jesus was popular,
not because of his parables,
but because of his mighty acts of kindness.

How could he not be popular?
He healed the sick and fed the poor,
and even ate and drank with sinners.
(Lk, 5:30-32)

But when the crowds heard his parables
they found themselves highly allergic
to the lessons they taught.

Meditation Prompt

The allergy still prevails.
Christian creeds, doctrines, and rituals
take no note of the parables.

The God you and I expect to meet face to face,
is an almighty God, a judge who goes by the book,
not the loving Father described by Jesus in
"The Prodigal Son" and "The Good Shepherd,"
two of his most beloved parables.
What's that all about? How can that be?

Author's Alert

The Parables are the best example
of the Bible as great literature.

The fact that some parables may not be exactly
as told by Jesus, matters little.

We can only deal with the hand dealt to us in the parables
since Jesus put nothing in writing.

64. MEDITATION

The Hidden Leaven

"The kingdom of heaven is like leaven
which a woman took and hid in three measures of flour,
till it was leavened."

(Matthew 13:33)

How odd of Jesus to say
the woman "hid" her leaven in the flour.

Was it because her leaven
is not the leaven of the Priests and Pharisees?

Was it because the bread she was baking
was not the unleavened bread of the Passover?

Was it because the bread in her hands
is the kingdom of heaven on earth?

The kingdom of heaven in this woman's hands
cannot be the kingdom of heaven in heaven.

The kingdom of heaven in her hands
is clearly not sexist Israel or sexist Christianity.

The man who told this parable
is clearly not the Jesus Christianity came to revere.

Meditation Prompt

In Genesis Chapters 2 and 3, the woman is last in being created.
and the first to sin. In Chapter 1 of Genesis Adam and Eve are created
at the same time and both are given dominion over the earth. Unlike
Judaism and Christianity Jesus favors Genesis chapter one in telling
this parable.

It is the woman's input that will make the bread of the kingdom rise.
But she has to do it by stealth.

In telling this parable Jesus is as bold as brass.

65. MEDITATION

The Lost Coin

"Or what woman having ten silver coins,
if she loses one of them, does not light a lamp,
sweep the house, and seek carefully until she finds it?
When she finds it, she calls together her friends and neighbors,
saying, 'Rejoice with me, for I have found the coin that I had lost.'
Just so, I tell you, there is more joy in the presence of the angels
of God over one sinner who repents."
(Luke 15: 8-10)

The "Or" that introduces this parable
links it with the parable of the lost sheep.

The Shepherd/Woman parables
are both metaphors for an unsinkable divine love.

Both parables cast doubt about the traditional belief
that God's love turns to wrath a nanosecond after our death.

Both parables are equally effective metaphors for infinite love,
but are not equally renowned as such.

Even as early as the writing of Matthew 18: 10-14
only the parable of the Good Shepherd is told.

Even in Christianity today in the good old U.S.A.
it is not officially permitted to image God as a woman.

Meditation Prompt

I do not know how God satisfies her justice
while never giving up on relentless divine love.
I do not try to explain how justice can be satisfied
if the God we meet is as described in these parables.
I simply trust that God has a way that is incomprehensible to us.
I trust in the infinite power of infinite love.

"O the depth of the riches and wisdom and knowledge of God!
How unsearchable are his judgments and how inscrutable are his
ways!"

(Romans 11: 33)

66. MEDITATION

The Motherly Father

" ...How many of my father's hired hands
have bread enough to spare, but here I am
dying of hunger! I will get up and go to my father,
and I will say to him, 'Father, I have sinned against
heaven and before you; I am no longer worthy to be called
your son; treat me like one of your hired hands.'
So he set off and went to his father. But while he was still
far off, his father saw him and was filled with compassion;
he ran and put his arms around him and kissed him."

(Luke 15: 17-20)

In this seemingly absurd parable
the father has gone too far,
killing the fatted calf for a prodigal son,
a son who squandered his inheritance on prostitutes.

The prodigal son, bad as he is,
is too good to be true.
He returns not because he expects a fatted calf banquet
but only out of love for his Father.

The faithful son, good as he is,
is exposed as not being so good.
He regrets his years of fidelity.
Why be faithful when infidelity is so richly rewarded?

The faithful son bitterly berates his father:
"I have never disobeyed your command,
yet you have never given me even a goat
so that I might celebrate with my friends."

177

Those hearing this parable,
both then and now, can only ask:
How can God almighty rule planet earth
as a motherly, rather than as an almighty, Father?

Meditation Prompt

My "love" of the Father may be bogus.
I may be mistaking "obedience" for love.
I may be motivated more by great expectations than by true love.
Sometimes those who behave badly
learn to love God while those who follow all the rules do not.
At least that is what Jesus teaches in this parable.

67. The Emotional Householder

"For the kingdom of heaven is like a householder
who went out early in the morning to hire laborers
for his vineyard. After agreeing with the laborers
for a denarius a day, he sent them into his vineyard....

When those hired about five o'clock came, each of
them received the usual wage. Now when the first
came they thought they should receive more; but
each of those also received the usual daily wage."

(Matthew 29: 1-2 & 9-10)

For the Galileans who heard this parable,
both laborers and householders,
the generosity of the householder made no sense.

For the householder it was a generous decision
to pay a fair wage to the first hired
and the same wage to the last hired.

But it was an unreasonable and dangerous precedent
to give to those who worked all day
the same wage as those who began work at the end of the day.

Man is a rational animal.
Reason, and not emotion, must prevail
in the distribution of wealth.

The householder in this parable
seems to act foolishly and recklessly,
even in our enlightened society today.

Meditation Prompt

What seems foolish to us is wisdom to Jesus.
Like his Father in heaven he saw a great deal of good
to be gained by such foolish generosity.
Nurturing that spirit seems to be in keeping with his mission
of ushering in his kingdom on earth.

68. The Good Samaritan

"And behold, a lawyer stood up to put him to the test, saying,
'Teacher what shall I do to inherit eternal life?' ...
He said to him, 'What is written in the law? How do you read?'
And he answered, 'You shall love the Lord your God with all your
heart, and with all your soul, and with all your strength,
and with all your mind; and your neighbor as yourself.'.....
But he, desiring to justify himself, said to Jesus, 'And who is my
neighbor?'"
(Luke 10: 25-29)

Jesus answered him with the parable of the Good Samaritan: (Luke
10: 30-37)

Imagine Jesus telling this parable
in the pre-civil rights deep South,
during a Christian Sunday worship service,
the most segregated hour of the week.

In those days
Many a southern baptized Christian
despised the African Americans
as much as the Galileans despised the Samaritans.

Would Jesus dare
make the hero of his parable
an uppity successful African American,
the equivalent of the Samaritan in this parable?

Would this Christian congregation stand up and sing
"We have a friend in Jesus" after hearing this parable,
in answer to the congregational question:

"Teacher, what must we do to inherit eternal life?"

Meditation Prompt

"God waits on human history
and suffers as she waits."

Eckhart

69. MEDITATION

The Pharisee and the Publican
or
The Teacher and the Tax Collector

"Two men went up to the temple to pray, one a Pharisee and the other a tax collector.
The Pharisee stood and prayed thus with himself, 'God, I thank thee I am not like other men,
extortionists, unjust, adulterers, or even like this tax collector. I fast twice a week, I give tithes of
all I get.' But the tax collector, standing far off, would not even lift up his eyes to heaven, but
beat his breast, saying, 'God be merciful to me a sinner!' I tell you, this man went down to his
house justified rather than the other.' " (Luke 18: 10-14a)

Little is more reassuring
than taking satisfaction for not committing sins
one has not been tempted to commit.

Extortion, injustice and perhaps even adultery
are likely more common temptations
among tax collectors than among teachers.

Little is more tempting
than the temptation to lift one's self up
by putting another down.

For example, take a favored Christian chant,
popular from Good Friday until recent times:
"We are the chosen people, you are not!"

Meditation Prompt

"Look at them at home; you will see them
with one hand hoisting the cap of liberty,
and with the other flogging the slaves."

Charles Dickens

70. MEDITATION

The Unforgiving Servant

"Then his lord summoned him and said to him, 'You wicked servant! I forgave you all that debt because you besought me; and should not you have mercy on your fellow servant, as I had mercy on you?' And in anger his lord delivered him to the jailers, till he should pay his debt. So also my heavenly Father will do to every one of you, if you do not forgive your brother in your heart."

(Matthew 18: 32-35)

The debts in this parable are given in terms of denarii and talents. Translated into today's terms the king forgave a debt of 100 million dollars while the servant was unwilling to forgive a debt of 100 dollars. As in The Lord's Prayer, debts are not about money but about our emotions.

A community in which Christians forgive others
as God forgives them,
would be the kingdom of God on earth.

If the Lord's Prayer and this parable
are not calls to action,
I don't know what is.

Though we Christians today
have no hope of ushering in the kingdom on earth,
we can begin with the kingdom within us.

Even pursuing that kingdom,
limited as it is,
is no walk in the park.

I have never found it easy
to think kindly of, let alone forgive, those
who trespass against me.

Truth be told,
my fantasy is to seize them by the throat
And cry out: "Pay what you owe."
(Matthew 18:28)

It is not uncommon for me,
while taking a walk on a fine sunny day,
to torture myself ruminating about some trespass against me.

Meditation Prompt

All too often good fortune, health, and weather,
as well as the kingdom of God within me,
have been squandered, thanks to the disgrace
of being an unforgiving servant.

Pardon the Interruption

A Not So Easy Essay

Never had Jesus been so angry.
God's baby, the kingdom on earth, was about to be aborted.
No abortion could be more blasphemous.

The abortionists were Pilate's lackeys, the priests and elders who opposed him, and his disciples, those who worked for him. To the priests and elders he tells the parable of the wicked tenants.
To his disciples he tells the parable of the wasted talents and the last judgment.

It is unsettling to see the incarnation of divine love ending his life in anger.
What made the man, who preached often against anger, end his mission in anger?

His kingdom mission in Galilee had captured the religious imagination of the people.
Multitudes came to hear him preach and see him tend to the sick and the poor.
In the story of his entrance into Jerusalem the Jewish people greet him with hosannas and palms.
What happened to trigger the frightening wrath revealed in his last three parables?

Matthew tells us it was his visit to the Temple. With whip in hand, Jesus put a stop to temple worship by freeing the animals ready to be sacrificed. Then he dared to call the temple, "a den of thieves." Why so was explained in Isaiah 1: 11 and 17:

" 'What to me is the multitude of your sacrifices?, says the Lord;
I have had enough of burnt offerings of rams and the fat of fed beasts...

seek justice, rescue the oppressed...' "

This was a condemnation of ritualism not Judaism.
Money spent on rituals is food taken from the poor. Surplus capital belongs first to them.

Such thievery abounds among the devout because of the fear that God is in constant need of ritual reassurances of his glory and his power. What should be feared is the love of our Father for his children who are most in need. This is the lesson of the last parable of Jesus, the parable of the judgment of the nations: Treat the least as if they were me or go straight to hell, no excuses accepted. (Mt. 25: 31-46)

This is not to say that we should wallow in guilt, a sinister emotion posing as a virtue.
But our world needs a Christianity that has not tuned out the last three parables of Jesus.

It is truly right and just that we reflect on one of the most teachable moments in history.

71. The Wicked Tenants

The chief priests and elders

(Matthew 21: 33-43)

In this parable, a householder plants a vineyard, entrusts it to tenants to take care of it, and then goes to another country. At harvest time he sends his servants to harvest what he planted. The first ones sent are beaten and killed, and so, too, the second group of servants. Finally, he sends his son who is also killed. What will the owner do when he returns, asks Jesus. His audience says he will put the miserable wretches to death. No, says Jesus, they will not be killed but they will pay the price for what they have done.
"Therefore, I tell you, the kingdom will be taken away from you, and given to a nation producing the fruits of it." (Mt. 21:43)

The wicked tenants in this parable
are not "the Jews"
but their religious leaders.

The chief priests and elders,
like the Vichy French government,
were the lackeys of an occupying power.

Even lackeys
enjoy the vestiges of power,
and oppose any who would take it away.

Jesus is never even-handed
when putting down the mighty,
paying no heed to any good they may have done.

He goes for the jugular,
reminding them how those in power

either beat up or kill the prophets sent by God.

As a prophet sent by God,
Jesus stood up to pious bullies
and struck at the heart of darkness.

Meditation Prompt

"There is a lag between the end of an age
and the discovery of the end. The denizens
of such a time are like the cartoon cat
that ran off the cliff and for a while is suspended,
still running, in mid-air, but sooner or later
looks down and sees there is nothing under him."

Walker Percy

72. The Buried Talents

The disciples who work for Jesus
(Matthew 25: 14-30)

A property owner going on a journey entrusts his money to the men
who work for him, giving more to some than to others. On returning
he praises those who did well but condemns the servant who did
nothing but sit on the little money given him, because he was afraid,
believing him to be a severe man, a man who reaps what he does not
sow. If you knew that, said the owner, you should have been afraid to
be lazy. To those who stood by he said:

"So take the talent from him, and give it to him who has
ten talents. For all those who have, more will be given, and they will
have an abundance; but from those who have nothing, even what
they have will be taken away. As for this worthless slave, throw him
into the outer darkness, where there will be weeping and gnashing of
teeth."
(Mt. 25: 28-30)

Never has laziness
provoked such a threat,
one allowing for no excuses.

Alone with his co-workers
Jesus is madder than hell,
And rightly so.

He is about to go on a journey,
arranged by Pilate,
by way of three nails and two planks of wood.

His valuable estate,
the kingdom of heaven in Galilee,

is to be entrusted to his co-workers.

In his heart he knows
they will not tend to his property,
the kingdom of God in Galilee.

They will not take up the cross he carried,
the cross of his ministry,
fearing that he is too demanding.
(He is Jesus, they are not.)

Meditation Prompt

Who will Jesus praise today?
Who will he condemn?
What is it that his followers do that Jesus calls "doing nothing"?
See his last parable in the next meditation.

73. The Judgment of the Nations
The Last Parable

(Matthew 25: 31-46)

"When the Son of Man comes in all his glory, and all the angels with him, then he will sit on the throne of his glory. All the nations will be gathered before him, and he will separate people one from another as a shepherd separates the sheep from the goats, and he will put the sheep at his right hand and the goats at his left. Then the king will say to those at his right hand, 'Come, you that are blessed by my Father, inherit the kingdom prepared for you from the foundation of the world; for I was hungry and you gave me food, I was thirsty and you gave me something to drink, I was a stranger and you welcomed me, I was naked and you gave me clothing, I was sick and you took care of me, I was in prison and you visited me.' "

Then the righteous will answer him, 'Lord, when was it that we saw you hungry and gave you food, and thirsty and gave you something to drink? And when was it that we saw you a stranger and welcomed you, or naked and gave you clothing? And when was it that we saw you sick or in prison and visited you? And the king will answer them, 'Truly I tell you, just as you did it to one of the least of these who are members of my family, you did it to me.'

Then he will say to those at his left hand, 'You that are accursed, depart from me into the eternal fire prepared for the devil and his angels; for I was hungry and you gave me no food, I was thirsty and you gave me nothing to drink, I was a stranger and you did not welcome me, naked and you did not give me clothing, sick, and in prison and you did not visit me.'

Then they will also answer, 'Lord, when was it that we saw you hungry or thirsty or a stranger or naked or sick or in prison, and did not take care of you? Then he will answer them, 'Truly I tell you, just as you did not do it to one of the least of these, you did not do it to me.' And these will go away into eternal punishment, but the righteous into eternal life."

Meditation Prompt

The Last Parable and the Lord's Prayer should be the Christian Creed, and should have been much more revolutionary than the Communist Manifesto.

We should not wallow in guilt, a sinister emotion posing as a virtue. We should, however, feel remorse and regret for the harm done to ourselves and our planet. But most of all we should begin to revere Jesus because, before dying, he entrusted to us his kingdom mission not because by dying he satisfied the terrible wrath of God.

A Not So Easy Essay

Jesus told his last parable about those enslaved in poverty shortly before his last supper, a ritual meal remembering the liberation of the Jews from the poverty of slavery. At that meal he set his table to feed those who treated the wretched as if they were Jesus.

Christianity re-set the Jesus table as the food of personal salvation for all who believe in Jesus as Lord and Savior. That is why in Christian tradition Jesus' last supper has nothing to do with his last parable. And that is why Jesus' last parable is not cited in Christian sermons on hell, nor in its doctrines and creeds.

The word "hell" in his parable to the nations is not a proper noun like "Detroit". If it were we would all end up in hell. It is, however, a metaphor Jesus relied on heavily in predicting the hell on earth that will be created by the Nations – a prediction that has been fulfilled:
War is hell and all we have known is peace between wars.
Poverty is hell and we have lost the war on poverty.

This parable was told to change the order of society, to reverse the rules by which we and our nations live. If we are to have a kingdom of God on earth, as prayed for in the Lord's prayer, the nations must pay heed to this parable. Politics must give more than lip service to Jesus' religious spirit.

But who can blame the nations? Christian prelates betrayed the nations by burying this parable, while priding themselves on preaching Jesus as being all about the kingdoms of heaven and hell. They have made its citizens the children of a lesser god, children who are kept in line by lures and threats. Will our prelates ever repent this betrayal? Will they proclaim publicly and officially from their hell-singed pulpits:

There is no hell, there never was and never will be a hell

as long as our God is Infinite Love. We do not know how
God satisfies the demands of justice without a hell,
but that is God's problem not ours.

There is no hell but the hell we create on earth.
We do this by not treating the least as if they were Jesus.

Meditation Prompt

"Only a donkey does not change its mind."

Moshe Dayan

"The Christianity they believe in is like the skeleton of a butterfly
caught in a spider's web; it contains only the external form;
the blood and flesh are gone."

Shusaku Endo

Meditation Prompt for chapter nine:

Jesus' Public Square Parables

"…I cannot help thinking that any religion
which begins with a thirst for immortality
is damned as a religion from the outset.

Until a certain spiritual level has been reached,
the promise of immortality will always operate
as a bribe which vitiates the whole religion,
infinitely inflames those very self-regards
which religion must cut down and uproot…"

C.S. Lewis

Author's Alert

Some revered Christian texts can take on new meaning when read
in the light of Jesus' last parable.

Revered text: "For God so loved the world that he gave his only son,
so that everyone who believes in him may not perish
but may have eternal life." (John 3:16)

New meaning: To "believe in him" could mean to believe
in treating the least as if they were Jesus.

++++++++++++++++++++++++++++++++++

Revered text: "I am the light of the world. Whoever follows me
will never walk in darkness but will have the light of life."
(John 8:12)

New meaning: To follow Jesus may mean to walk the walk he
walked, and carry the cross he carried, not the one Pilate put
on his back, but the one he took up in his ministry.

++

Revered text: "I am the way, and the truth, and the life.
No one comes to the Father except through me."
(John 14:6)

New meaning: The only way to the Father is the way Jesus took,
hallowing the Father's name, doing his will,
working for the kingdom of God on earth.

N.B. "New meaning" does not mean "only meaning" but
only what the text can rightly mean to me or you.
Citing texts as proofs has been the mortal sin of our tradition.

Epilogue: Nathan and Paul

Nathan

The best parable man in the bible

After King David had sex with a warrior's wife he sent her husband
into battle,
one in which he would surely be killed. (2 Samuel 11: 14-15)

With no hesitation whatsoever,
no hemming and hawing,
Nathan told king David this parable.

Nathan did something Jesus never did
when he told his parable to a king,
a powerful and highly revered king.

Jesus' pregnant mother
may have had Nathan's parable in mind
when she predicted her son would put down the mighty.

And why not?
Nathan's parable is the best in the bible.
No audience was more revered, no trap more clever.

Nathan's Parable: (2 Samuel 12: 1-9)

" 'There were two men in a certain city, the one rich the other poor.
The rich man had many flocks and herds, but the poor man had but
one little ewe lamb, which he had bought. He brought it up, and it
grew up with him and his children; it used to eat of his meager fare,
and drank from his cup, and lie in his bosom, and it was like a
daughter to him. Now there came a traveler to the rich man, and he
was loath to take one of his own flock or herd to prepare for the

wayfarer who had come to him, but he took the poor man's lamb, and prepared that for the guest who had come to him.' Then David's anger was greatly kindled against the man. He said to Nathan, 'As the Lord lives, the man who has done this deserves to die; he shall restore the lamb fourfold, because he did this thing, and because he had no pity.'

Nathan said to David, 'You are the man! Thus says the Lord, the God of Israel: I anointed you king over Israel, and I rescued you from the hand of Saul; I gave you your master's wives into your bosom, and gave you the house of Israel and of Judah; and if that had been too little, I would have added as much more. Why have you despised the word of the Lord, to do what is evil in his sight?' "

Meditation Prompt

Where is the man or woman today who could so judge a pope, a president, a preacher or a politician as effectively as Nathan? What a blessing that would be!

Paul

The Anti-Parable Man in the bible

Before his name change to Paul
Saul persecuted the Jewish followers of Jesus,
a Jew determined to knock Jesus out of Judaism.

After his vision and name change
Paul stood up to Peter, James, and John,
a convert determined to knock Jesus out of the Jesus movement.

Those who were chosen and taught by Jesus,
the supposed acknowledged leaders,
meant nothing to Paul. (Galatians 2:6)

"For I want you to know, brothers and sisters,
that the gospel that was proclaimed to me...
I received it through a revelation of Jesus Christ."
(Galatians 1:11)

"...nor did I go up to Jerusalem
to those who were already apostles before me
but I went away at once to Arabia..."
(Galatians 1:17)

"Then after three years I did go up to Jerusalem
to visit Cephas (Peter)
and stayed with him fifteen days."
(Galatians 1: 18)

Only fifteen days! I can imagine Paul
storming into his meeting with Peter, crying out:
"I came not to praise Jesus but to bury Jesus."

And bury Jesus he did, preaching only Christ crucified and risen;
relying on his own parable: (1 Corinthians 15:22)
"...for as all die in Adam, so all will be made alive in Christ."

Jesus in the crucified and risen Christ meant everything.
Jesus in the least meant little to Paul.
The parables of Jesus meant nothing to Paul.

Meditation Prompt

According to Paul, Jesus was born to be crucified.
As Redeemer he paid Satan's ransom demand.
As Savior he saved us from the wrath of God.
Paul, not the parables, shaped Christianity today.

Appendix

1. Some Uncommon Observations

2. The Lord's Table, a home ritual

"Poverty tells the Church she has not been up to the mission inaugurated by Jesus – that she must be bolder in answering his call to a true sense of history and a true sense of humility."

Cardinal Lecaro

"Ministry is doing something for the advent of the kingdom, in public, on behalf of the Christian Community."

Thomas O'Meara, O.P.

"The most astonishing revelation about Jesus
is not that he got the job done
but that he cannot get it done without us."

J.F. La Croce

1. Some Uncommon Observations

GOD

♦   Before creation there was only God. The cosmos is the first revelation of God. It reveals that self-love is not enough even for God.

♦   God was behind creation, but so far behind that this presence is barely perceptible. God did not create the world by saying let there be this and let there be that.

♦   Planet earth is not God's classroom where all take a pass/fail test and most of humanity fails it.

♦   God's kingdom will come on earth; God's will *will* be done on earth as it is in heaven.

♦   What God has put asunder in mystery no one can join together in doctrines. Neither Creeds nor sacred scriptures can trump the mystery. The ways of God are incomprehensible.

♦   God's book is a book of stories, told by two great communities of faith, told in the days when it was believed God did "his" business only through men.

♦   Long gone are the days when God could rightly be imagined as "Lawman", as an almighty white guy with a beard.

♦   God is present to us as infinite love not as a judge who goes by the book.

Which book that would be is still being debated.

- ◆ Belief in God as the architect and CEO of hell is the blasphemy of blasphemies. What Father could be more cruel?

- ◆ The word "hell" is a metaphor not a proper noun. Hell is not a place, like Detroit.

- ◆ If the word "hell" in Jesus' last parable were to be taken literally we would all end up in hell. See Matthew 25: 31-46.

- ◆ How God satisfies the demands of divine justice without a hell is God's problem, not ours. But be assured. God can handle it. With God all things are possible.

- ◆ God is not an easily offended touchy-tetchy God. Nor does God suffer from poor self esteem, craving elaborate ritual affirmation. (Jesus believed God is offended when too much is spent on rituals.)

JESUS

His creed,
the Lord's Prayer and Last Parable,
should be our creed.

His vision,
the kingdom of God on earth,
was meant to disturb the dreams of the nations.

His style,
more country crier than creator of creeds,
was more like the Buddha than the Christ.

His prayer,
naming the evil we do as trespasses against one another,
took the spiritual sting out of God's reactions.

His baptism,
committing him to the kingdom on earth mission
had nothing to do with heaven or hell.

His life,
lived mostly as an anonymous Jew,
features his humanity not his divinity.

His death
was the worst possible defeat,
not the best possible victory.

Jesus should have lived a long life;
he would have used the years well;
his kingdom mission would have been better served.

Jesus was nothing like you would expect.

All rabbi Jesus needed for his mission was a good pair of legs,
hands that had the gift of healing, and some mind-boggling parables.

All gentle Jesus needed, to take a whip in hand,
was to see money taken from the poor and spent on rituals of worship.

Of the three unique incarnations of God, Jesus, Moses, and
Mohammed, only Jesus did not have an army.

James F. La Croce

Christianity

Christianity is a house divided,
and not one of these houses
can claim to be the kingdom of God on earth.

Laws give structure to vision.
Creeds give it a voice and rituals celebrate it.
The problem with Christianity is in its vision.

We Christians have become the children of a lesser god,
A god who keeps us in line
by the threat of punishment and the lure of rewards.

We Christians did not choose to follow
the religion practiced by Jesus,
but a religion about Jesus.

The eyes of Christianity
are on the kingdom of heaven as the prize
while those of Jesus were on the kingdom on earth.

Christianity's use of the bible as a book of proofs,
has made it a house divided against itself,
and demeans the faith of others.

A world becoming one by the marvels of mass communication,
and not by the grace of marvelous conversions,
can no longer tolerate traditional Christianity.

The world today needs a Christianity
which relies on the Lord's Prayer as its creed
and the last parable as its guiding light.
(Mt, 25: 31-46)

Even the most noble Christian traditions,
promoting love for one another, for family and country,
seem selfish and even sinister in light of Jesus' ministry and last
parable.

Jesus set his last supper table
to feed those who minister to the least,
as if they were Jesus.

Christians re-set the Jesus table
to feed their souls
and so assure their personal salvation.

2. The Lord's Table

(A home ritual)

The Lord's Supper was for many years a home ritual, much like the Passover ritual. Nothing could be more traditional than the Lord's table being a home table. It is not unreasonable to suppose that the owner of the home presided at the table, blessing and distributing the bread and wine, even if the owner was a woman.

The Lord's table was a table not an altar, a table set by Jesus to feed those who would carry his cross, the cross of ministering to the wretched and the poor. What we Catholics call the altar of sacrifice could rightly be called the table of compassion. The following is a suggested home ritual.

+++++++++++++++++++++++++++++++

The Table of Compassion

<u>Opening Prayer</u>

You commanded us to carry the cross of your ministry,
but our church, country and culture has taught us otherwise.
Grant that in some way we may become co-carriers with you
in completing the kingdom mission entrusted to you by our Father.

<u>Public Confession</u>

We confess our evil acts,
not as sins against you, our God,
but as trespasses against one another.

We believe these trespasses
will be forgiven,
but only as we forgive one another.

We confess, sorrowfully and regretfully,
that we have wrongly revered you
as touchy and tetchy about how you are worshipped.

We confess, with sorrow in our hearts,
that we have not treated the least
as if they were Jesus.

O Lord, we feel remorse and regret
for harm done to ourselves and others,
but deliver us from feelings of guilt,
a sinister emotion posing as a virtue.

Lord have mercy on us.
Where guilt prevails love fails.

Readings:

How chosen is decided by those present.
Gospel readings should be favored.
All should be aware that Gospels are holy stories not hard facts,
and were written to encourage belief not prove belief.

Quiet Time

Profession of Faith

We believe in God,
an incomprehensible mystery
who is neither male nor female.

We believe in the universe,
the first incarnation of God,
the revelation that even for God self-love is not enough.

We believe in Jesus,
beloved son of God,
sent to usher in God's kingdom on earth.

We believe in that kingdom on earth,
and that belief is the rock
on which we stand as a community.

Above all, we believe
that we are not the children of a lesser god,
one who relies on lures and threats.

The Lord's Prayer

The Sign of Peace (all embrace as warmly as appropriate to the
temperament of those present)

Blessing of the Bread and Wine
(by all present or any of those present, female or male)

Be with us O Lord, as we do this in memory of you:

Take this bread all of you and eat it: THIS IS MY BODY.
Take and drink this wine all of you: THIS IS MY BLOOD.

Communion Prayer

By eating this bread and drinking this wine may we in some way
be an answer to your prayer to our Father; may his kingdom come on
earth.

Quiet Time

(All are invited to dance the dance of compassion)

Used with permission from Willa Bickham of Viva House, Baltimore Catholic Worker.
Quote used in the artwork is unknown to the artist.

CPSIA information can be obtained at www.ICGtesting.com
Printed in the USA
BVOW010038041212

307197BV00001B/58/P